Writing Science Research Papers - An Introductory Step-by-Step Approach to A's

2nd Edition

BIOTECH PUBLISHING
P.O. Box 1032 Angleton, TX 77516-1032
http://www.biotechpub.com

Writing Science Research Papers - An Introductory Step-by-Step Approach to A's
2nd Edition

by David B. Williams

Published by Biotech Publishing
P.O. Box 1032
Angleton, TX 77516-1032

printing 10 9 8 7 6 5 4 3 2 1

Publisher's Cataloging in Publication Data

Williams, David B.
Writing Science Research Papers -
An Introductory Step - by - Step Approach to A's
2nd Edition

Second Edition
PN101 808.06
Incudes index, charts, glossary
1. Authorship - Handbooks, manuals, etc.
2. Scientific writing - technical writing
Library of Congress Catalog Number: 99-067937

ISBN 1-880319-14-4 Softcover
Cover by Tammy Crask

Contents

Dedication

This book is dedicated to all science teachers who struggle to motivate and interest their students in the "joys" of research. And to all my former students who struggled to produce the "perfect" research paper. Finally, to my daughter, Elisabeth, and her friends who endured the trials, frustrations, and triumph of science projects and to my son, Nathan, who one day will face the same fun!

Acknowledgements

I would like to thank my colleagues at Emmanual Christian School for their support. To Jim Sample for the science -fair preparation he provides for his students. To Linda Dickerson, a fellow "project enthusiast" who has strived with me to pull the best from her pupils. A special thank you to Mrs. Mallow for her critical evaluations. And finally, a deep felt apprectiation to Mr. Tant for his confidence that this book would fill a real need and without which it might never had been published.

A Note From the Publisher...

When we first saw this book, it was in the form of a guide which David Williams was preparing to help his own students with science fair project presentations. As a semi-retired science teacher, I recognized its potential of becoming the book for which I had yearned for twenty years.

The popularity of the initial edition has resulted in further expansionfor this new second edition. A whole new chapter is dedicated to use of internet resources. Explanations of charts and tables have been amplified and new practice exercises included.

There are many excellent style manuals for graduate students and practicing professionals, but they leave unanswered the questions of beginning students. Often, many do not know the terminology of scientific writing, and almost all are intimidated with their first attempt to use the indexes to scientific literature. The oft asked question, "How do I begin and what do I do?" is clearly and simply answered in an early section that provides a guided tour through library research.

Author Williams has expanded his work to explain more about literature reviews and has included examples of his requirements and grading criteria. The latter, as they stand, will serve many teachers; others will modify them to meet their own special needs. Students will appreciate having them as a clue to what is expected.

English teachers often complain that they receive little, if any, training in the special conventions of writing for different scientific disciplines. Hopefully, they will find this book of value when their students ask for help.

Many others recognize the need for early training in scientific writing. College professors fume over the lack of preparation of both undergraduate and graduate students. Research managers in government and industry express frustration about the shortcomings in communication skills of otherwise technically competent professionals.

The answers are here. David Williams has provided not only the "how-to" for the preparatory student, but also a valuable review and reference tool for the practicing scientist or engineer who did not have the benefit of this book while in school. He might well have titled it STRESS PREVENTION.

Section I.

An Introduction

Section I

WHAT IS A SCIENCE RESEARCH PAPER?

Many students react with horror when they hear the term,"science research paper." Their dread arises from lack of familiarity with good scientific writing. The problem is complicated by difficulty in finding out how to write a paper that will be acceptable to both science and English teachers. Good scientific writing has many special requirements that expand on the basic principles of English composition.

There are two types of science research papers. The first is often called a literature review. Its purpose is to compile and summarize scientific research about a particular topic. The author does no laboratory investigation for the review. Some reviews are very extensive and may cite hundreds of reports in the scientific literature.

The second type of research paper is one prepared to describe a specific investigative project done by the author. A good paper of this kind usually includes an abbreviated literature review as part of its background information. Additionally, it will contain the researcher's hypothesis, descriptions of materials and methods, experimental results, and discussions of those results.

This book is intended to be a guide and a tool to understand and to execute a top-grade scientific research paper. It is not intended to be a grammar text nor an exhaustive guide, but an outline of one method and format for writing a scientific paper. While written primarily for the student just beginning to learn about scientific writing, it will also, hopefully, provide a useful review and reference for the professional scientist or engineer. The flow chart on the next page summarizes the steps involved in scientific research writing.

Many resources and tools are the same for both the review and the project report. These will be described first. Then we shall study the literature review which becomes part of the research project report. Doing it this way will keep you from having to read the same thing twice!

Research Paper Overview

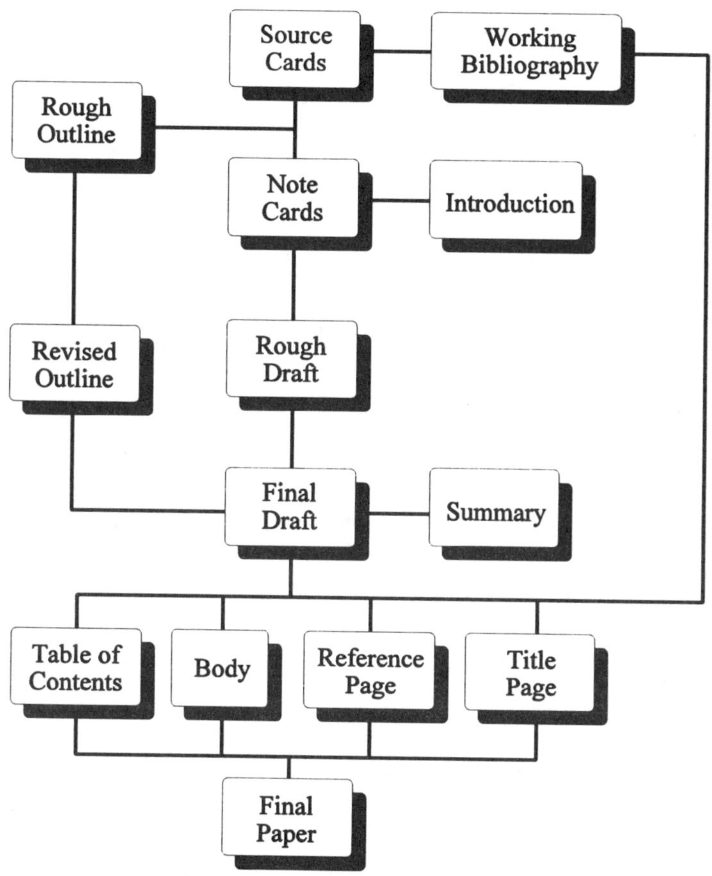

Section II.

The Tools And Resources

Chapter 1

HOW DO I START?

The key to an excellent research paper, and the spin-off benefits of an award winning science project is a thorough search of the scientific literature published about your particular topic. By knowing the literature, you become the expert in your chosen field of study. This acquired expertise is important when discussing your paper or project with science fair judges, your instructor, or the general public. If a specific subject has not been assigned, Chapter 9 provides some guidelines for choosing a topic. These apply equally to a literature review and a project report.

The first step toward becoming the expert is to search for and digest large quantities of information, and boil it down into an easy to handle package called "the research paper." Researching provides the opportunity to discover what other investigators have published concerning your topic. No one will deny that this is hard work. However, by the time your final polished draft is submitted you will be able to stand and speak confidently about the topic.

The first step is choosing a subject. If a specific one has not been assigned, Chapter 9 provides some guidelines for choosing a topic. These apply equally to a literature review and a project report.

Where Do I Look?

Once you have selected a subject, the next step is searching for the place to begin. Sources of information are plentiful. Here is a sample of places to search:

1. **Books: college textbooks, comprehensive works, and monographs**
2. **Science encyclopedias**

---

3. **Laboratory manuals - many contain concise background information**
4. **Scientific and professional journals**
5. **Abstract journals - short article summaries**
6. **Handbooks - compilations of information on many topics**
7. **Audio tapes and videos**
8. **Thesis abstracts**
9. **Interviews with the experts**

Still the question arises: "how do I find the information?" Aside from interviews with experts, the list above looks like trips to the library. Many of the resources may be unfamiliar, so we shall explore them in detail in the next chapter.

Chapter 2

SOURCES OF INFORMATION--USING THE LIBRARY

A good place to start would be the library computer. Most large library systems, colleges, and universities have computerized search systems where a topic (subject) or key word is entered and the computer searches for the match-up. Generally this method will help locate the topic among books in circulation or help locate a broad topic on the shelves. Then you can search for particulars. Many libraries have computerized other information such as periodical and abstract indexes.

Encyclopedias Give Clues

Another avenue is to use scientific encyclopedias to familiarize yourself with the topic or gain enough information to narrow the search (or expand the search with other key words you can try in the computer search). Many times the articles written in an encyclopedia will refer to other related topics that will shed more light on the subject. Besides providing information, scientific encyclopedias will have references cited at the end of the entry. Use these to further expand the search.

General topical encyclopedias such as the ***Encyclopedia Britannica*** are useful for obtaining background information, an understanding of your topic, and even outlining ideas. Do not depend on the encyclopedia for in-depth research. Excellent research goes far beyond copying from a general encyclopedia. Look for good scientific encyclopedias available in many libraries. Some encyclopedias of scientific merit include:

Encyclopedia of Chemical Technology
Grzimeks Animal Life Encyclopedia
McGraw-Hill Encylopedia of Science
Plants and Earth Science

Be sure to check avaliability of the new CD-ROM encyclopedias at your library. These range from general references such as the ***Grollier Encyclopedia*** to very specialized subjects such as the ***Encyclopedia of U.S. Endangered Species***. The latter is a good example of how much information can be put on a CD-ROM. Over 700 species are described in detail.

Handbooks

Most major sciences have handbooks which contain brief descriptions and data about a specific topic such as a chemical compound or a physics equation. Many times, handbooks cite references that may prove valuable for further research. Two classic examples are the ***CRC Handbook of Chemistry and Physics*** and ***The Merck Index***.

Scientific Journals

Books are only a part of the research. For most quality research efforts, the bulk of good current information will come from scientific journals and magazines. Articles from research journals can take three forms:

1. **A full paper**
2. **A note**
3. **A communication**

Full papers are complete reports on a research project. They will include a short abstract (summary) written by the authors of the research, full experimental detail, and discussions. A note, on the other hand, will be a final report on a project. It will include some experimental details, but not an abstract.

The communication is a preliminary report on a finding of unusual merit or importance. It is short with little or no experimental detail, but will be followed by a full paper at the completion of a project.

Magazines of questionable or poor scientific merit should be avoided. These might include general news magazines, general reading magazines, special interest publications, "pop" science magazines, and newspapers. There are hundreds of reputable professional scientific journals. Some of the more common ones, which will be found in most libraries, might include the following:

American Biology Teacher
American Journal of Physics
Child Development
Environmental Science Technology
Journal of Agricultural and Food Science
Journal of American Psychology
Journal of Chemical Education
Journal of the American Chemical Society
Journal of the American Medical Association
Nature
Science
Scientific American

Source Location

Public libraries have many books to help in your research. However, most library systems are limited in the number and kinds of professional journals to which they subscribe. Not having journals does not necessarily prevent you from researching. Most libraries subscribe to periodical indexes of scientific journals. Two widely found indexes include:

The General Science Index - **contains thousands of article citations relating to nearly any topic in science.**

The Social Science Index - **contains thousands of article citations relating to psychology, animal and human behavior, and human development.**

Most colleges and universities have very in-depth indexes that may prove invaluable. Some may be computerized in combination with several other indexes. Many have brief abstracts of the papers. A few of these are listed below:

The Agricultural Index - **plant and animal research**
Chemical Abstracts - **thousands of chemistry related citations**
Psychology Index - **an expanded version of the** *Social Science Index*
ERIC - **educational related research**
Biotechnology Index - **expanded version of The** *Agricultural Index* **(CD-ROM)**

If you have not used abstracts or indexes before, they may look large and intimidating. Don't worry! The editors of the best ones have provided clear and simple examples and illustrations for their use. These will usually be found on the inside cover or near the front of the volume. A few minutes spent with them will save hours of time later. Figures 2.1 - 2.4 provide examples. They are reprinted with permission of leading publications in different scientific fields.

Excerpta Medica
FORMAT OF ABSTRACT

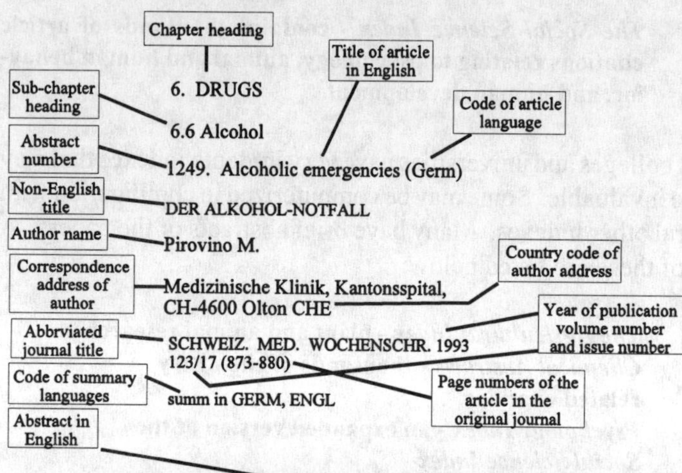

Gastric lavage, intestinal charcoal decontamination and specific drug antagonism, therapeutic measures widely applied in other intoxications, are of no clear benefit or unavailable in patients with alcohol intoxication. The gastric first-pass-effect is important in modifying the kinetics of alcohol, and clinically relevant drug-alcohol interactions occur in situations of both acute and chronic alcohol abuse. Alcohol-induced hypoglycemia and ketoacidosis should be considered in every severley ill alcoholic patient. The recognition of alcoholism is important and rewarding, since therapeutic action by the practicing physician can be of significant help.

Figure 2.1. Instructions for Excerptia Medica; ©1994, Elsevier Science B.V., Amsterdam

Psychological Abstracts

Key to the Text

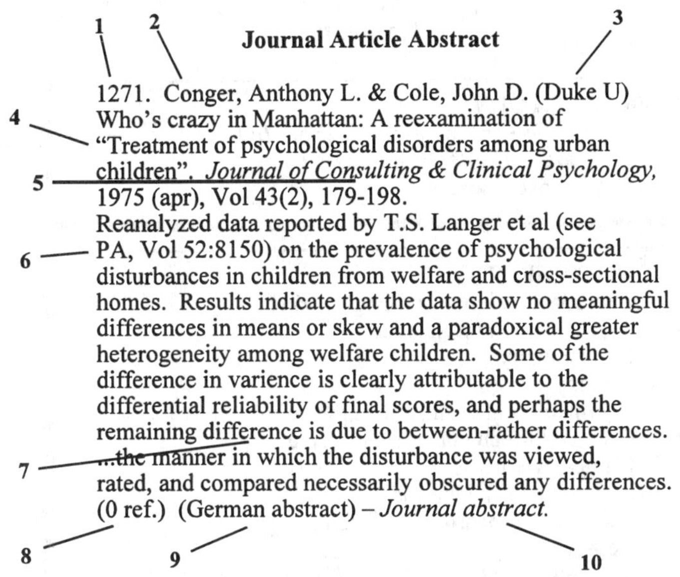

1 - Record number.
2 - Author(s) or editor(s). Journal records: As many as four are listed; if there are more, the fourth is followed by "et al." Succession marks (i.e., Jr., II, III, etc.) Are not given.
3 - Affiliation of first - named author/editor only.
4 - Article, book, or chapter title, including subtitles, or series titles.
5 - Primary publication title & bibliographic data.
6 - Reference to a previous entry in *Psychological Abstracts.*
7 - Text of serial abstract.
8 - Zero references included
9 - Abstract languages are indicated if they are different from the language of the original article.

Fig. 2.2. Instructions for *Psychological Abstracts,*
© 1994, American Psychological Association, Inc.

Conference Papers Index
Vol. 22, No. 3 May 1994
Coden: CPIND7

Contents

Fig. 2.3. The self-explanatory contents layout of *Conference Papers Index*, © 1994, Cambridge Scientific Abstracts

Biological Abstracts

Subject Context	Keyword	Ref. No
Nal variations among	**Scorpion** Toxins centroides-suff	107366
protein composition of	**Scotch** Pine buds in different period	101431
inerea rhizoctonia-sp	Pine douglas-fir climate soil	105524
sphoprotein ripening	Scotland UK/Phosphorus Metaboli	100223

Searching Procedure

1. Determine subject words to be searched. Check spelling, adjective forms, synonyms, British spelling and the Abbreviations List on the following page.
2. Locate words alphabetically in the KEYWORD position.
3. Consult words to the left and right of the KEYWORD position for additional information.
4. Using reference numbers, consult individual entries.

Fig. 2.4.The Subject Index (Specific Words) is one of four indexes in *Biological Abstracts* (BA), © 1994, by Biological Abstracts, Inc. The others are an AuthorIndex (Personal or Corporate Names), Biosystematic Index (Taxanomic Categories), and Generic Index (Genus-Species Names). Note procedure 4 in the example--the reference numbers apply to the entries, not pages.

A word of warning: Beware of general periodical indexes in the libraries. Most of the articles cited in them are of questionable scientific merit and usually originate from popular, nonscientific periodicals. Much information in these kinds of periodicals is "second guesses" about someone else's research. Generally they are undocumented. If in doubt, check with your instructor before using articles from general periodical indexes.

Most colleges and universities will not permit non-enrolled students to check out books and magazines, just as reference materials cannot be checked out of public libraries. However, you can photocopy as many articles or pages of a book as you need. Just remember to write all the bibliographic information about the magazine or book from which you copy. Most importantly, be certain to photocopy the reference page of any article or book chapters you copy. The references cited in the text of the articles are listed at the end of the article. If you copy pages from a book, the citations are generally listed either at the end of the chapter or the end of the book itself. Many books list articles and publications of related interest. These listings can carry your research even further.

The key to good research is neither to become overwhelmed by the amount of information available nor become frustrated if at first you do not locate enough information. Remember, the very nature of research is to search and search and "re-search" until you find what is needed.

Chapter 3

MAKING BIBLIOGRAPHY AND NOTE CARDS

The working bibliography is a collection of books, magazine articles, and other information (collectively called sources) needed for the paper. Bibliography information is written on 3x5 or 4x6 index cards, using one card per source.

A working bibliography is not static. As libraries are searched for good information, some sources will be more useful than others. It is not unusual to discard a source as you find newer ones that provide better in-depth knowledge. Don't be afraid to have too many sources. It is far better to have too many than not to have an adequate number of books and magazines. For instance, several journal articles may have the same topic information as a single book but convey the information in a more condensed form. Avoid shallow or vague sources or ones that only repeat the same information gleaned from a previous source.

Don't be disappointed if there are not entire books about your topic in the local library. More than likely, an index search of a general topic book will turn up more specific information than searching for a book title on your subject. A computer search for books may not bring up titles of your topic, but it can provide a general location of books on the shelf. Go to the shelf and do a "finger search" through the book's index to find specific information on your topic.

Once sources have been selected, it is helpful to photocopy important pages, especially if the sources are reference books and cannot be taken home. Take your sources and discuss them with your instructor. Afterwards, begin transcribing the bibliographic information - author, title, volume (or edition), and publisher - to 3x5 index cards. Systematically number the sources, both the index card and any photocopies.

Refer to the example bibliography cards in Figure 3.1 to help determine what information, per source, is required. Pay attention to punctuation since the final reference page in the research paper must be correctly punctuated.

When writing bibliography cards, be certain to record ALL the information needed. It will save hours of agony when the book you need is not on the shelf or the article was accidentally thrown away. It is even advisable to write the information on any photocopies made of journal articles or parts of a book and then make a card (the photocopy becomes an emergency backup).

Book Card

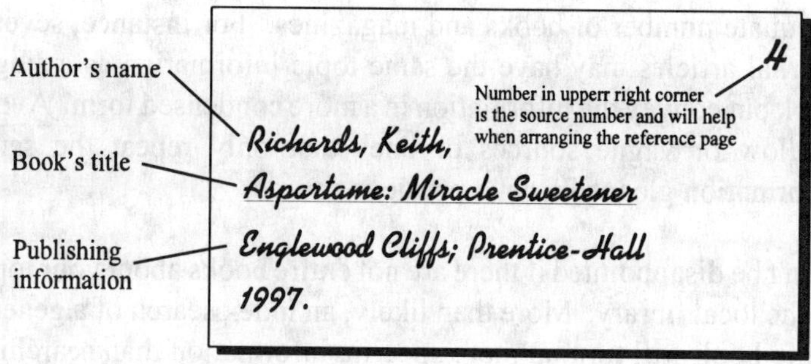

Figure 3.1. Bibliography Card

Periodical Card

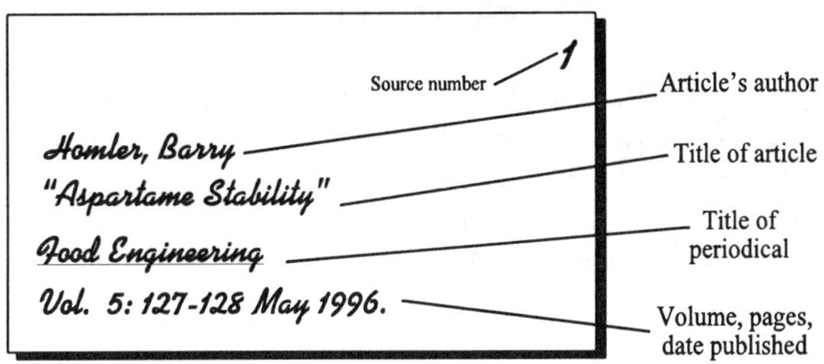

Encyclopedia Card

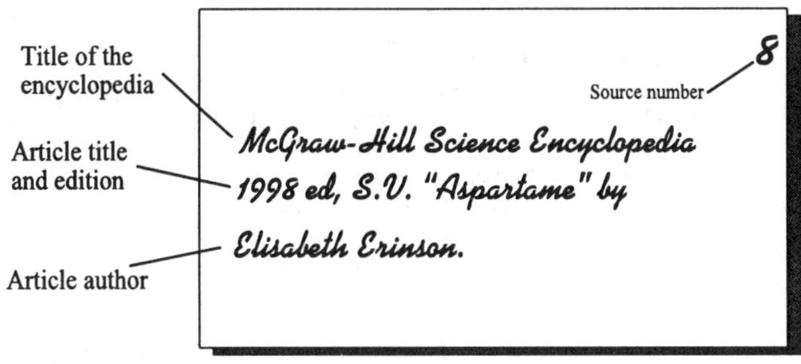

Figure 3.1. (cont'd)

Chapter 4

USING THE CD-ROM

If you use a library which has CD-ROM databases, you will find that computer searches make the task of reviewing a subject much easier. Some index publications provide for printouts of abstracts about your topic. Teachers and science fair judges may or may not consider these acceptable in place of traditional hand-written note cards. Ask.

With just a little practice, CD-ROM databases make searching easy, as you will see in the following example. It is from a student guide provided by the M. D. Anderson Library of the University of Houston. Other good libraries provide similar help keyed to their specific conditions.

Why would you search CD-ROM databases?
CD-ROM databases are simply indexes on computer. However, searching CD-ROM offers several advantages. CD-ROM databases are updated more quickly than printed indexes; you may search for articles under several keywords rather than just one subject heading; you can combine multiple concepts; you can print out your results on paper. Many CD-ROM databases include an abstract (summary of journal article) like our example below.

Example: from Eric CD_ROM subject search: College Applicants.

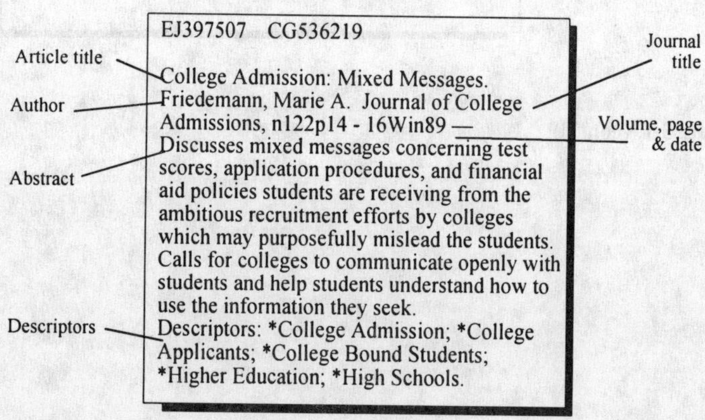

EJ397507 CG536219

College Admission: Mixed Messages.
Friedemann, Marie A. Journal of College Admissions, n122p14 - 16Win89 —
Discusses mixed messages concerning test scores, application procedures, and financial aid policies students are receiving from the ambitious recruitment efforts by colleges which may purposefully mislead the students. Calls for colleges to communicate openly with students and help students understand how to use the information they seek.
Descriptors: *College Admission; *College Applicants; *College Bound Students; *Higher Education; *High Schools.

Chapter 5

INTERNET RESOURCES

Since the first edition of this book was published, there has been an explosion of electronic communication. An inherent part of new technology is a new language, new ethics, and new rules. The technical progress of the internet and e-mail has created a mass of confusion in scientific writing. The various professional scientific organizations, librarians, and English teachers have yet to establish a firm set of rules acceptable to all.

Internet access has become almost a necessity for students doing research for serious scientific writing. Libraries have severely cut back on their subscriptions to scientific journals because of unbelievable cost increases. Professional scientists as well as beginning students are having to rely on electronic communication. Unfortunately the good has been accompanied by the bad.

BE CAREFUL! There is lots of garbage and special interests masquerading as legitimate science. Safe sources are peer-reviewed electronic journals, government agencies, most colleges and universities, and well known organizations such as the American Cancer Society. Be especially wary of individuals and unknown societies which represent themselves as being the only source of new or secret research.

Your school or teacher might have specific guidelines for referencing electronic sources. If not, the following are some general rules and cautions.

Citations and References

In the text, cite internet sources as you would any other, either by numbering or the author/date system. E-mail deserves a special word of caution. Obviously, you should respect the privacy of e-mails sent between individuals. Do not quote or cite without permission. Even if the e-mail is an informative one posted to a discussion group, courtesy requires requesting permission to quote.

References are written essentially the same as any others except for the additional inclusion of the URL.

Writing Style Mechanics

Writing internet URL's and e-mail addresses can sometimes present problems. Most are preventable by being consistent in style with a few rules.

1. Use italics for both e-mail addresses and URL's. Doing so helps avoid confusion with other sentence elements.

2. With very few exceptions all letters should be lower case.

3. Do not use internal space in addresses. Punctuation marks are used to separate elements.

4. If the address is continued to a second line, do not use a hyphen to show the continuation. It could be confused for an element of the address. Instead, break addresses with the units that begin them as
   http://
   www.biotechpub.com
   Always carry a dot or @ down to begin the next line as
   services
   @biotechpub.com

5. A period is permissible after an address at the end of the sentence.

The New Language

Nowhere is the evolution of our language more evident than in electronic communication. New words have been invented to describe new processes; in other cases, the meaning of older words has been modified.

Many persons are still intimidated by computers or for other reasons dislike electronic communication. A major reason for this might be the overall poor, often intelligible, writing found in software manuals. Do not assume, as many manual authors do, that your reader is conversant with the language used. Avoid or explain specialized technical terms.

Computer enthusiasts have further complicated our understanding by developing new slang terms to describe their activities. These usually have no place in scientific writing.

A Big Trap Awaits

The language of computer technology like that of biochemistry has become replete with acronyms and abbreviations. These are appropriate to shorten and simplify the reader's task, but be sure to define them on first usage for the uninitiated.

Be careful to avoid the trap of saying it twice. There are easy redundancy kinks in many acronyms. Here are some common examples.

DOS - The S is "system." Avoid "DOS system."
CD - The D is "disk." Avoid "CD disk."
RAM - The M is "memory." Avoid "RAM memory."

A Final Thought

The internet is not a library archive. What is there today may be gone tomorrow. URL's change without warning. Home pages are frequently modified or replaced. In citing internet sources, be sure to give readers enough information so that they will have some hope of finding the original sources if changes occur.

Chapter 6

GET YOUR ACT TOGETHER: THE REPORT OUTLINE

Outlines are both the "skeleton" and the foundation of the research paper upon which all research information is built. A good outline gives direction, cohesiveness, orderliness, and conveys information in a concise fashion - all the elements of a well written paper. While a carefully thought out "skeleton" does not guarantee an excellent paper, it will make writing the final draft much simpler.

The key to an excellent outline is being descriptive, but brief. Take large bodies of information and reduce them to simple, brief "bullet statements." Then, organize them in a step-by-step description of the research topic to take the reader from the beginning to end without distractions, detours, or repetitions.

When writing the outline, use your sources to organize the sequence of ideas and information believed to be important to the paper's development. Lay out the sources, then pick and choose the best ones to build the outline. Jot down a descriptive phrase or sentence from selected sources to later develop into outline points and subpoints. It is a good practice to make marginal notes on the rough outline, referring to the sources containing information important to that part. The use of source numbers will save time locating materials once note-taking begins. Use a general encyclopedia for ideas about organizing the topic.

The minimum requirement for most research papers is three to five major sections with two to four subpoints and, in some cases, two or three sub-subpoints. Use the outline to build your discussion and keep the paper from straying into useless information or bogging down in repetition.

When writing the outline, make a preliminary scheme, jotting down key points you wish to cover. Rearrange information to find the way your thoughts are most clearly conveyed. Add points as needed or delete points if it is apparent the topic is too broad. Use the outline to narrow down the topic or work toward an "information goal" (focus). Don't be satisfied with the first outline. Set it aside for a time and then come back and re-write it (or better yet, let someone else read it).

Figures 5.1 - 5.2 show model outlines which illustrate the ideas of brevity and direction. They also show double and single-spacing differences. Note that all the items are brief and to the point. Also, notice that no questions are used.

Table 6.1.
Summary of points to remember when writing the outline.

1. Be brief, use "bullet statements", not cumbersome, long sentences.
2. Avoid the use of personal pronouns such as you, yours, my, we, I, or ours. Think "3rd person"
3. Never refer to the topic as "it". Refer to the topic in proper descriptive terms.
4. Avoid the use of questions such as "What does Metamorphosis Mean?" Questions generally sound awkward.
5. Use scientific terms when writing the outline.
6. Don't write like you speak.
7. Keep the margins straight and indent at each level of the outline. Use a 5 space indention. (1 centimeter if handwritten.)
8. After writing the initial outline let someone else read it. Give it a rest and then rewrite it.

Once the outline is adequately developed, the next step is more note-taking in preparation for "fleshing out" the skeleton.

I. Insect Developement

A. Simple Metamorphosis

1. Egg
2. Nymph stage
3. Adult stage

B. Complete Metamorphosis

1. Egg and larva
2. Pupa stage
3. Mature adult

II. The Mosquito

A. General Information

B. Life Cycle of the Mosquito

1. Egg “fafts”
2. Larva (wriggler) stage
3. Pupa (tumbler) stage
4. Adult mosquito

C. Behavior of Adult Mosquito

1. Food location
2. Mating habits

III. Mosquito and Environmental Factors

A. Environmental Stress

1. Alkaline conditions
2. Acidic conditions

B. Selected Studies of Stress Factors

Figure 6.1. Example Outline- Double-spaced

I. Introduction
II. Chemical Description of Aspartame
- A. Composition of Aspartame
- B. Decomposition by Substitution
- C. Products of Decomposition
  1. L-a-aspartyl phenylalanine
  2. Diketopiperazine

III. Aspartame's Stability and Kinetics
- A. Factors Affecting Stability
  1. Time
  2. Temperature range
  3. PH range
- B. Mechanisms of Decomposition

IV. Select Studies on Decomposition Products
- A. Tsang, Clark, and Parrish (1985)
- B. Stamps and LaBuza (1989)
- C. Hayakawa, Schilpp, and Wong (1990)

I. Introduction and Background
II. History of Sunspot Observations
- A. Chinese
- B. Western Astronomers
  1. Scheiner
  2. Galileo
  3. Herschel
  4. Langley

III. The Sunspot
- A. Origins of Sunspots
- B. Descriptions of Sunspots
  1. Temperature
  2. Parts of a sunspot

IV. Sunspot Cycles
V. Sunspots and Sun Rotation
- A. Differential Rotation
- B. Rotation Speed and Latitudes

Figure 6.2. Example Outlines - Single-spaced

Note-Taking and Note Cards

Note-taking involves reading whole paragraphs of information and boiling out the main ideas or points. The best method of note-taking is to first match the source with the outline and cover each point in a systematic fashion. Record the key idea or the direct quote on a 4x6 lined index card. Be certain to head the card with a word or phrase to aid in the correlating of notes on the outline. It is also a good idea to jot down, on the card, its point of location on the outline. The concepts and information written on the note card should be your own words and your organization of ideas.

Direct quotations are many times the best way to convey the meaning or concept presented in the literature. Be careful not to overquote a source. Doing so gives the reader a feeling of having a "cut and paste" research paper.

When taking notes, it is not a good practice to copy whole paragraphs and simply change a word or two; this can lend itself to charges of plagiarism. It becomes quickly evident to the reader if sources are copied word for word from a book or magazine, especially if you make reference to some previous portion of a source ("...as discussed in chapter 5...") or make mention of something you have not covered up to that point in the paper. The goal of note-taking is to rewrite ideas and information in your own organization and style, not to paste together copied portions of different sources!

Table 6.2.
Ten Tips for Note Taking

1. Use 4x6 lined index cards for writing notes.

2. Before starting, record the source number on the upper left or right corner (the source numbers should correspond to bibliography cards).

3. Write a word or phrase on the top line to show where notes appear in the outline of paper.

4. Write a brief summary or direct quote from the source you are using with one card per idea or quote.

5. Should a summary or quote require more than one card, number each card consecutively in the opposite corner from the source number.

6. On the bottom line, record the page number from where the source notes came.

7. When taking notes, try to avoid quoting the source. Paraphrase the quote whenever possible.

8. Don't copy the source word-for-word. Again, paraphrase the main ideas in your own words.

9. After the notes are completed, arrange them in the order of the outline using the headings from the note cards.

10. Don't try to reproduce diagrams, tables, and charts on note cards. Make a note on card of items you wish to add in the final draft. Assign figure or table numbers as you go to save confusion later.

The next two pages, Figure 5.3, are quick reference summaries of tips for taking notes.

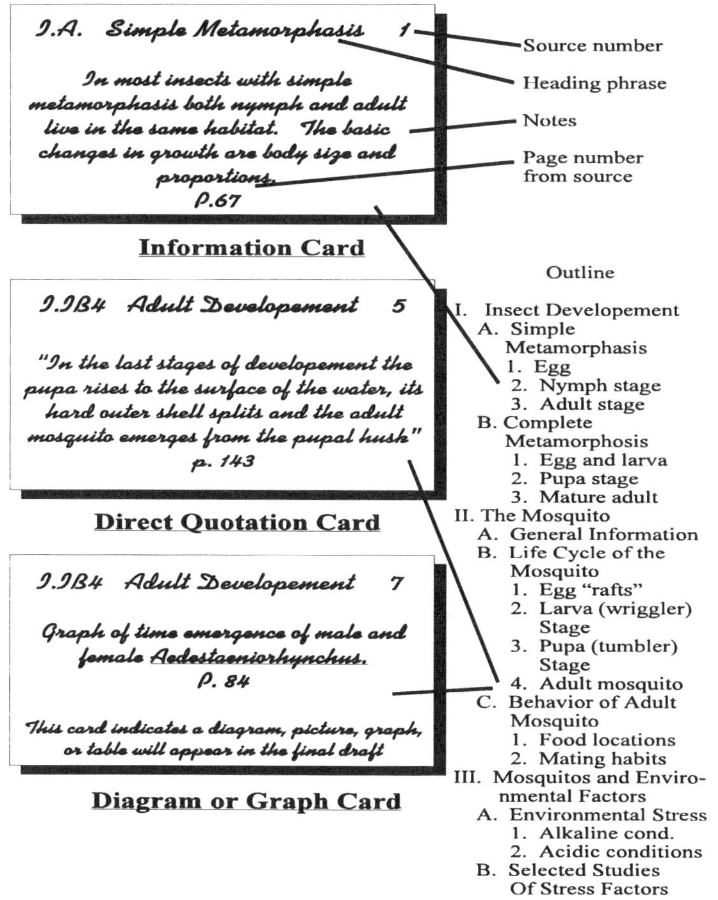

Figure 6.3. Example Note Cards

IIA Composition of Aspartame 1

Aspartame, L-a-aspartyl-L-phenylalanine menthyl este (APM) is a dipeptide made up of two amino acids: L-a-aspartic acid and L-phenylalanine menthyl ester.

P. 127

Information Card

IVC Selected Studies 2

"NDA-CN derivatization methods were helpful for sensitive determination of Asp, Phe, and AP by enhancing their sensitivity, and thereby better protection of Aspartame's degradation products."

P. 1260

Direct Quotation Card

IIIB Mechanisms of Decomposition 5

Diagram showing the mechanism for the formation of the anhydride containing species of APM. (Photocopy to be added later)

p. 432

Diagram or Graph Card

I. Introduction

II. Chemical Description of Aspartame

A. Composition of Aspartame

B. Decomposition by Substitution

C. Products of Decomposition

1. L-a-aspartyl Phenylalanine
2. Diketopiperazine

III. Aspartame's Stability and Kinetics

A. Factors Affecting Stability

1. Time
2. Temperature
3. PH range

B. Mechanisms of Decomposition

IV. Select Studies on Decomposition Products

A. Tsang, Clark, and Parrish (1995)

B. Stamps and LeBuza (1989)

C. Hayakawa, Schilpp, And Wong (1996)

Figure 6.3. (Cont'd)

After note cards are written, they can be arranged in the order in which the information appeared in the outline (another reason for having good outlines). Remember, the outline can be revised and re-structured at any point as new information is added.

Note cards can also be disregarded if the outline is revised and the information is no longer needed or better information is obtained later.

Chapter 7

WRITING THE ROUGH DRAFT

The rough or preliminary draft is not a single entity, but is actually made up of several discreet parts involving many processes. There are at least seven parts and processes that go into finalizing the preliminary draft:

1. **Organizing the note cards**
2. **Writing the introductory paragraph**
3. **Transforming note cards into a coherent, intelligently written body of information**
4. **Footnoting or citing sources properly**
5. **Integrating support material (pictures, diagrams,tables, etc.)**
6. **Writing a summary paragraph**
7. **Preparing the reference and further reading page**

Each of the seven aspects will be described in more detail in the next several pages.

The first draft is the organizing and writing of the research paper from the note cards. It is usually written in pencil (if not typed on a word processor), on every other line, using wide rule paper to facilitate editing notations and writing corrections into the text. After it is written, the paper should be set aside to be later re-read and re-written until it makes sound scientific and Grammatik sense.

The process of writing begins by organizing the note cards according to the sequence of the outline. Proofread the cards since they are likely to contain errors or missing information as a first writing. It may be best to break up the paper into small sections, starting with the introduction, rather than attempt to write the whole thing in one sitting. The best way to proceed is to follow the sequence of the outline to insure continuity and cohesiveness. Use transition sentences to tie together the several sections. Finish one major outline point, set it aside and take time to reorganize the note cards for the next point. Have photocopies and books ready in case there is a question about the notes. This will also help if something new must be added to help round-out the information or aid in tying together several subpoints.

Introductory Paragraphs

After organizing your note cards, begin the paper with an introductory paragraph which acquaints the reader with the research paper. It prepares the reader by giving a preview of information the paper covers. The introductory paragraph should highlight the main points of the paper. Usually the main points of the outline can be tied together into a few descriptive sentences and used as an introduction.

Sometimes a research paper will begin with a statement of fact about the topic, followed by a summary of the main points taken directly from the outline. This method is very effective in grabbing the attention of the reader. It also indicates maturity in writing style. If you decide to include a scientific fact in the introductory paragraph, be sure to give the reference. (Citations in introductory paragraphs are not uncommon in scientific writing.)

Here are four important points to remember when writing the introductory paragraph:

1. **Keep it brief, no more than 50-75 words in length (more, and it bogs down).**
2. **Be descriptive - focus on the main points or subpoints of information to be covered.**
3. **Be definitive - sometimes a key term can be defined in the introductory paragraph, or some important background information can be provided.**

4. **Be resourceful - don't overwork terms such as "describes" or "discusses." (Use a thesaurus to find other descriptive terms.)**

Read the sample paragraphs in Figure 6.1 for help or ideas on wording the opening paragraph. These illustrate different ways of prefacing the paper. Later, we shall look at using style in introductory paragraphs, to teach good writing skills.

Up to this point in the research paper, you have searched the literature, written a tentative outline, written bibliography cards, taken notes from the sources, and penned a tentative introductory paragraph. Now it is time to write the first rough draft.

Nearly half the citizens of the United States depend on groundwater for daily water needs. It, therefore, makes sense subsurface water supplies be contamination free. Unfortunately, this is not the case. Over the past three decades, there has been a proliferation of groundwater pollution which could endanger the health and well being of millions who depend on subsurface waters. The objective of this research paper is threefold: 1) to briefly describe groundwater, aquifers, and movement of groundwater through aquifer systems; 2) it will describe contamination of subsurface waters, including sources, transport, and fate of pollutants; 3) it will explain arrest and remediation techniques employed by environmentalists.

The following research paper will discuss several facts of the homologous series dioxin or polychlorinated dibenzo-p-dioxins (PCDD). The primary focus will be upon 2, 3, 7, 8 -tetrachloro-dibenzo-p-dioxin (TCDD) and its physical and chemical properties, its sources, and pathways into the environment. There will also be descriptions of several studies conducted on TCDD's.

The 1982 approval by the FDA for general use of the artificial sweetner, aspartame, created quite a stir among consumers. Here, at last, was an artificial sweetner having less than 1% of sugar's calories and taste nearly indistinguishable from sugar's. This research paper will describe some of aspartame's properties, its sustainability, and kinetics. It will also highlight studies pertaining to its decomposition products and quantitive techniques in determining those products.

Nearly one-half the number of children in hospital wards are there due to some kind of prenatal acquired malformation. The focus, of this research paper is to explore the impact of teratogeneous substance upon prenatal fetus developement. Three substances will be spotlighted: lead, mercury (and related compounds), and PCB's (polychlorinated biphenyls). All three substances are considered extremely dangerous environmental pollutants and ones not usually consciously induced.

Figure 7.1. Introductory Paragraphs

Writing Guidelines

The rough draft, following the outline, is the organizing of note cards and writing the research paper for the first time from those cards. The first, or preliminary draft should be written and re-written until it meets sound scientific and grammatical criteria. Allow at least a full week (two weekends) to write the paper. If you have a calendar, refer to it for due dates and criterion guide-lines for other information.

The general guidelines for structuring the paper are as follows:

1. **Use wide rule paper, not college rule.**
2. **Write or print in pencil.**
3. **Write on every other line (if using a word processor, double-space).**
4. **Write or print on the front side of paper only.**
5. **Begin the paper with the introductory paragraph.**
6. **If you are not using the word count function of a word processor, use a numbering system to help keep track of the number of words written:**
    - A. **Count 25 words, above the 25th word write "25" with a circle around the word. (See example in Figure 6.2.)**
    - B. **Count 25 more words and write the number "50" above the word and circle the word. (See Figure 6.2.)**
    - C. **Continue counting words by 25's until you reach the end, where you will write the number for the last word.**
    - D. **Footnotes, tables, graphs, and charts are not included when counting words.**
7. **Don't end the paper with the words "The End."**
8. **Consult a leading science journal in your area for guidlines regarding numerical representation.**
9. **Be certain you reference your sources (citations and documentation will be covered later).**

10. **Practice good writing skills. Do not write like you speak - a good paper requires a more formal presentation.**

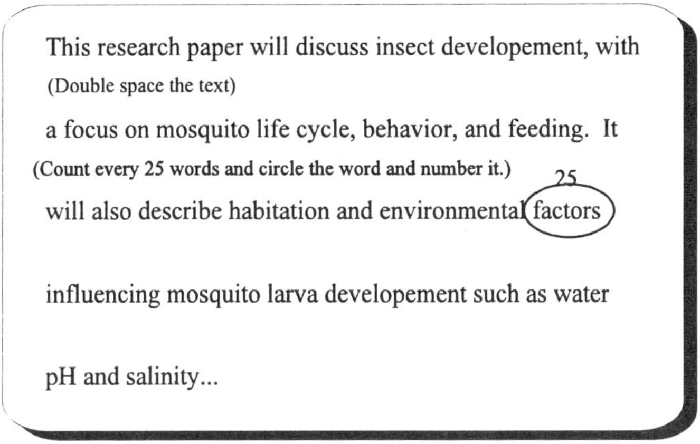

This research paper will discuss insect developement, with

(Double space the text)

a focus on mosquito life cycle, behavior, and feeding. It

(Count every 25 words and circle the word and number it.) 25

will also describe habitation and environmental factors

influencing mosquito larva developement such as water

pH and salinity...

Figure 7.2. Counting the words

The important rule for writing is to be able to convey the facts and information in an organized, concise, and "readable" fashion. The importance of a previous point justifies saying it again: Never write like you talk; it sounds unscientific and generally violates good grammar. The following information will be helpful when writing your own paper.

Remember that contrary to common English usage, scientific information is usually presented in the third person passive voice. Avoid the use of pronouns as much as possible. Some pronouns that should not appear in the paper include: I, my, me, our, you, yours, us, and we. Restructure the sentence to say the same thing without using the pronoun. For example:

My research paper will describe the properties of aspartame...

could be rewritten as:

The following research paper will describe the properties...

Another example of restructuring a sentence:

We can write the process of decomposition of aspartame as a chemical equation.

could be restructured as:

A chemical equation can be written to summarize the decomposition of aspartame...

Avoid the use of unscientific terminology. There is no room in scientific writing for slang or infantile terms. Use scientific terms whenever possible. Many times a thesaurus can help locate a word to substitute for a less desirable term. Table 1 lists some possible substitutes for commonly used unscientific words. Keep in mind that this list is not exhaustive. You can possibly think of more suitable terms than those suggested.

Similar to oversimplified terminology is "over-worked words." These are words used over and over in a paragraph. Refrain from using a term or phrase too often in a paragraph (it sounds repetitious and awkward.) A thesaurus of synonyms and antonyms such as ***Roget's College Thesaurus*** or ***Webster's Abridged Thesaurus*** should be used with a dictionary to help convey a thought or concept with intelligent language. Remember, do not write like you talk!

Table 7.1.
Rewording

Saying It Another Way

Common word or phrase	Saying it Intelligently
Deals with	Pertains to, relates to, concerned with.
Works	Performs, functions, operates.
Like (as in “likes a lot”)	Prefers, chooses, predilection.
Lot or lot of	Frequent, many, abundant, pervasive, predominate.
Best (as in “works best”)	Unequalled, greatest, profound affect.
Rest (as in “left-over”)	Remainder, the balance of.
About	Pertains to, applies to, regarding, in aspect to.
Used (”how its used”)	Operated, applied, utilized.
Show	Describe, capsulize, summarize.
Him (when describing both genders)	Them, they, child, adult, subject (as in test subjects).
Gives	Provides, furnishes, presents.
That, just	Omit whenever possible. It is considered verbal garbage (verbiage).

Introductory paragraphs are often written with overworked terms such as "describes." By substituting other expressions, the idea of "describing" can be presented without the repetition. Below is an example of a poorly written introductory paragraph followed by a more mature writing of the same paragraph.

My research paper will describe some of aspartame's properties. It will describe it's stability and kinetics. It will also describe several articles about it's decomposition products. And the last part will describe methods of measuring it's decomposition products. (38 words)

A few word substitutions and some restructuring produces a clearer opening:

The following research paper will describe properties of the artificial sweetener, aspartame. It will discuss aspartame's stability, kinetics, and decomposition products. In addition, several studies highlighting quantitative techniques for measuring aspartame's decomposition products will be reviewed. (37 words)

(Can you find other instances of mature writing style where a more suitable word or phrase was substituted?)

Writing style is especially important for scientific names used in the biological sciences. When writing scientific names for organisms, capitalize the genus name and use lower case for the species (or subspecies) names. Italicize the entire name. For instance, the scientific name for the house mosquito is:

Culex pipiens.

(genus)(species)

Italics should be indicated by underlining if an italic typeface is not available. This convention distinguishes the genus and species from other classification names. A species name is never used without the genus name preceding it.

Use Table 2 as a checklist to make certain that you have not committed some of the most common writing errors.

Table 7.2.
Writing Errors

Most commonly made errors in writing
Run-on sentences - Two or three complete thoughts in one sentence.
Lack of punctuation - missing periods, commas, and quotaion marks.
Parenthesis missing to end a parenthetical statement.
Paragraph indentations missing or ill-defined.
Nonsensical sentences, usually incomplete sentences or transposing two different sentences and creating a new sentence.
Incomplete citation - page number or date missing.
Changing tense from present to past or past to present.
Leaving words out of a sentence.
Fragmented sentences or incomplete thought
Inappropriate use of pronouns.
Overuse of verbiage such as "that" and "just".
Using unscientific terminology (see Table One)

Documentation and Citations

Even if the paper is reporting the author's research, it will include information from a multitude of authors pulled together and presented in a systematic fashion. Because a research paper borrows heavily from other researchers and scientists, it is extremely important to give credit for someone else's work.

To use someone else's writings without proper recognition is PLAGIARISM. Plagiarism is a form of theft. To take someone's work and pass it off as your own original research is stealing. Plagiarism could include the following:

1. **Borrowing a phrase, idea, or materials not your own**
2. **Using someone else's writing without proper use of quotation marks**
3. **Using another student's work**

To avoid plagiarism, usually a complete rewording is necessary. Changing a few words is not enough.

Beyond rewording, it may be necessary to rework the order of thoughts and ideas because borrowing someone's sequence of ideas and thoughts without proper credit is also a form of plagiarism.

When using the materials of other writers follow these guidelines:

1. **Acknowledge borrowed material within the text by using proper citations.**
2. **Enclose all direct quotes within quotation marks. Be sure to credit the source.**
3. **Make sure certain paraphrased material is written in your own style and language.**
4. **Provide a bibliography entry for every book or periodical that appears in the citations.**

During the writing, whenever a note card is incorporated into the text of the paper, decide whether a source citation should appear. Generally, use citations after transposing notes off several cards from the same source, and after several paragraphs of information taken from the same source. Also, cite a source after using a direct quote, employing support materials and data not of original design or collection (pictures, tables, graphs, etc.), and when making reference to someone's research by name or inference.

The numbering and frequency of citations will depend on the order and extent of borrowed ideas, the number of direct quotes, and the size of the working bibliography.

As the paper is written, make notes in the text if diagrams, pictures, tables, and graphs will be used. Keep track of diagrams, etc. in the text by referring to the note card number that contains them. Use phrases such as "...refer to Figure 1..." or "...see Table 3..." in the text of the paper to direct the reader's attention to it. You have the option to either cite the diagrams, tables, or pictures in the text when they are first mentioned or use a citation with them. (The Example Research Paper gives a sampling of both.) Cited information is not considered general knowledge. Numbers and statistics, tables, charts, diagrams, and figures must be credited to their authors as well.

Should you refer to other researchers (or make reference to their work) there must follow a citation and there must also appear a reference in the list of sources at the end of the paper. For instance, if you refer to Dr. Smith's study on mosquito larva, but do not actually use his information, you must still have Dr. Smith's study cited and referenced in the list of sources used. See Figure 6.3.

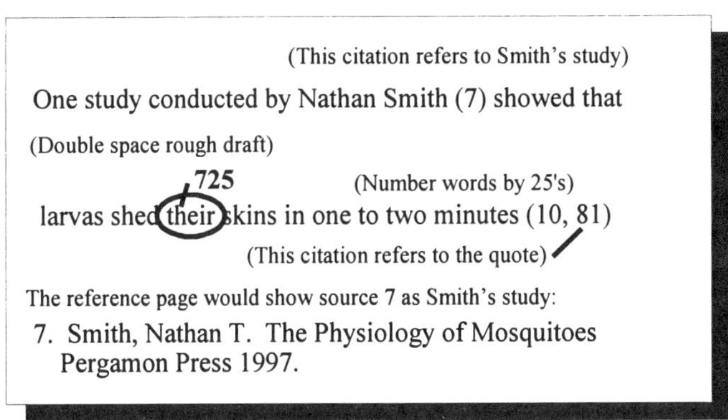

Figure 7.3. Scientific citation for unused source

Preparing a Citation

We have seen the importance of proper citations. It is now time to look at actually writing them into the text of the rough draft. Working with note cards aids in identifying the source to cite because the bibliography card number (source number) is written on the note card (Figure 5.3). Each time a note card is used, write down the source number and page number directly from the note card. A well written research paper is amply documented with many references.

Scientific Citation

When writing a scientific citation, place parenthesis around the entry. The entry must contain the source number and may include the page numbers. Check a journal in your field to see which convention it follows. If you are merely making reference to someone's work (such as Dr. Smith's study mentioned earlier) then a source number will suffice. See figure 6.4.

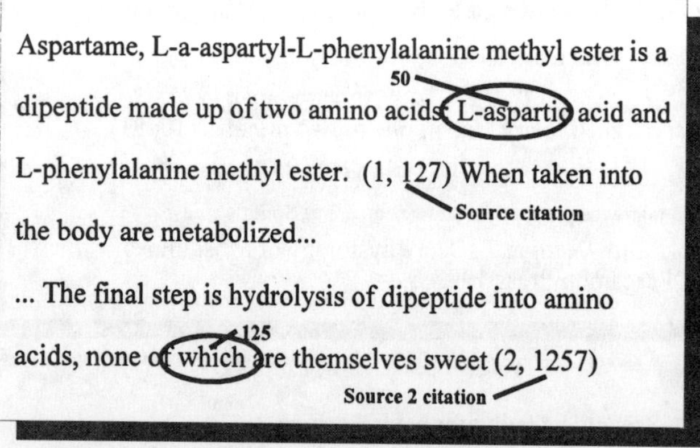

Figure 7.4. Scientific Citation

Author-Date (A-D) Citations

Those choosing a behavioral science topic follow a slightly different citation system that requires the last name of the author and the publication date. Many biology, biotechnology, medical, and agriculture journals also use it. This system is called the A-D system and does not require source number or page number. You will often find this system referred to as the A-P-A (American Psychological Association System). The reference page at the end of the paper is written differently as well. Instead of numbering the entries, the reference is entered alphabetically by last name.

"Biological gender is genetically and hormonally determined" (Golman, 1994)

(Author's last name and publication date)

Figure 7.5. A-D Citation, single author

The Summary

The last major hurdle in the research paper process is writing the summary paragraph and final draft.

The summary paragraph should be added to the rough draft before writing the final draft. This paragraph capsulizes in 50-75 words the main points of the paper and also makes a concluding statement so as not to leave the reader hanging in mid-air. In other words, the summary draws the paper to a tidy close.

To keep track of the number of words written, use a systematic numbering scheme as described previously. Then note the number of the last word in the summary above the last word. Do not try to squeeze in two words by insulting the reader's intelligence with "The End." Do not include captions from support materials, citations, or punctuation marks as part of the word count. However, numbers under 100, written out, can be counted. An illustration of word counting can be seen in Figure 6.2.

An easier way is available if you are using a computer. Simply activate the word count function of your word processing program and let the computer do it.

When writing the summary, avoid any statements of opinion and stay away from editorial comments about the topic. Keep in mind that the objective of the paper is to report facts and information, not write an editorial for the local newspaper. Also, try not to end the paper with a scientific fact unless it directly relates to some point in the text of the paper. Figure 6.6 shows some representative summary paragraphs.

A basic lesson from speech and journalism courses could be used here to summarize the approach:

- **Tell the readers what you're going to tell them (intro paragraph).**

- **Tell them (the body of information).**

- **Tell them what you told them (summary paragraph).**

Conclusion

It is hoped that through this brief overview, the reader will perceive the problem of groundwater contamination as being a complex mixture of groundwater hydraulics, the variety of contamination sources that directly impact groundwater quality, the complexity of the contaminants, and the availability technology needed for post-contamination treatment of subsurface waters. The intention, also, is to point to the immensity of the problem of subsurface contamination. What impacts one geographic location ultimately impacts other regions well beyond the source point of contamination.

This research paper has attempted to give mathematical descriptions to some of the key physical properties of dioxin (TCDDs) through discussion and evaluation of several key studies and reports published by environmentalists. These studies have touched upon solubilty, absorption, and environmental pathways. It is hoped the reader will gain some new insights into environmental fate of one of the most toxic man-made compounds known.

Conclusion

This brief paper described the physical and chemical properties of aspartame and its chemical stability – discussing the factors affecting its stability such as pH, time, and temperature. This paper then went on to describe the chemical degradation which aspartame undergoes to produce several hydrolysis products. Finally, it reported several key studies outlining various HPLC seperation methods in an attempt to quantify aspartame's decomposition products.

The implication for psychological and general human development will begin to emerge as scientific researchers and educators make meaningful contributions toward addressing the problems associated with prenatal exposure and maturation of the child. In studying teratogenic effects, general information of interest to psychology as a science may emerge. For psychologists interested in neurochemical and neuroanatomical factors as a key to behavior, it will also emerge as research continues to unlock the mysteries of teratogenic agents.

Figure 7.6. Example Summaries

Chapter 8

The Final Draft

After the preliminary draft has been carefully read and corrected by your instructor it will, no doubt, need further revision and correction to be shaped into its final version called the final draft. The final draft might include some or all of the items on the following list:

1. **Ensure that the summary paragraph was added.**
2. **Check for spelling errors (consult the dictionary if in doubt). CAUTION: If you are using a word processor spell checker, watch for typos which will spell another word such as "from" instead of "form," as these will not be recognized as errors by the computer.**
3. **Correct any grammar errors and restructure sentences. Table 2, page 40, lists common problems.**
4. **Ensure that paragraph separations are well defined.**
5. **Check citations and corresponding references.**
6. **Finalize the sequence of support materials. Add others your instructor suggests.**
7. **Write or type the title page.**
8. **Final proofreading: Recheck spelling, punctuation, citation agreement with reference page, and title page.**
9. **Write or type the auxiliary pages.**
10. **Photocopy the entire final draft.**

Table 8.1.
The Preliminary Draft at a Glance

1. Organize the rough or preliminary draft around the outline and note cards.
2. Write in pencil, double spaced on one side of the paper. If using a word processor: triple space.
3. Keep your sources handy to refer to in case problems arise or you want to add information.
4. Use transition sentences to connect major points or sections of the paper.
5. Begin the paper with the introductory paragraph (tell the reader what your going to tell them).
6. Add citations (footnotes) as information from note cards is transcribed to the paper.
7. Use good writing style and avoid slang or unscientific terminology.
8. Indicate in the rough draft location of diagrams, pictures, graphs, and tables (to be added in the final draft).
9. Set the finished rough draft aside for a few days then run it through a "critical reading".
10. Make corrections recommended by the "critical reader".
11. Add the summary (concluding) paragraph. (Tell them what you told them).
12. Count the words in the text either by 25's or 50's numbering every 25th or 50th word consecutively.
13. Review the section on writing the Reference Page and add your own.
14. Save everything (bibliography cards, note cards, outlines, etc.) Even after submitting the preliminary draft.

Integration of Support Materials

Whenever possible use a picture or diagram to clarify descriptions in the text. It is far better to use a diagram while explaining or detailing a process. For instance, when describing the internal organs of the mosquito it would be imperative to have diagrams of the internal structures showing relative position of organs in the insect's body. The old saying could never have more meaning: "One picture is worth a thousand words." This is not meant to suggest a diagram can count for 1000 words toward the minimum count!! There is no doubt pictures, tables and graphs enhance a research paper tremendously, and creative use of these support materials may often make the difference between a good or an excellent paper. Below are some helpful hints for the use of support materials.

1. **Use illustrations whenever you give detailed descriptions of structures, especially in the biological sciences.**
2. **Avoid lengthy data tables unless absolutely necessary.**
3. **Cite any diagrams, pictures, tables, etc. as if they were part of the report text.**
4. **In-text placement of diagrams, etc. is preferred; however, they can be added at the end of the paper provided they are clearly referred to in the paper (see model research paper for examples).**
5. **Carefully trim the diagram or picture and use RUBBER CEMENT or a UHUf stick to attach them to paper. (Many other glues wrinkle the paper.)**
6. **If needed, "white-out" the original caption and add your own.**
7. **Reserve a nice illustration for the report cover.**
8. **If time permits, photocopy the pages with attached illustrations and diagrams since glued items may peel off.**

Bibliography (References)

A research paper is only as valid as the extent of the working bibliography or references. If a citation appears in the text of the paper, but has no corresponding entry on the reference page, that authority is invalid and useless. It is very important to list every source used, even if it is a diagram or picture.

The most common mistakes in the reference page include the following:

1. **Not having an entry corresponding to a citation**
2. **Entries which have no corresponding citations**
3. **Incorrect entry format: forgetting to underline book titles, indenting the second line of entry (see example reference page)**
4. **Omitting the reference page altogether**

Many times authors make reference to a list of books or periodicals not actually used in their research writing. Generally, these are called "Further Reading" or "Suggested Reading." These are lists of materials of related interest. Feel free to include a "Further Reading" list after the reference page.

The term "bibliography" seldom appears in scientific writing. The list of sources actually used or referred to is generally called "List of References," "Literature Cited," or simply "References." In keeping with the best traditions of scientific writing, your paper should refer the reader to one of the following:

List of References
Literature Cited
References Cited
References
Sources Cited

References are listed numerically as they appear in the body of the paper. Citation 1, for instance, should refer the reader to source 1 on the reference page. Citation 2 should correspond to source 2 on the reference page, citation 3 should correspond to source 3, etc. The exception to this system is the A-D citation system referred to earlier. A-D reference pages are alphabetized by author's last name (the author's last name and date of publication appear in the citation).

Writing the reference page is a simple procedure because all the sources used in the actual writing are on index cards. It is only a matter of transcribing the information from the index cards to the reference page. Some word processor programs will generate the reference page from the text citations. Hopefully, the punctuation is correct on the cards, but if in doubt check a grammar book for clarification. Figures 7.1-7.2 illustrates both scientific and A-D reference pages.

Here is one final note on reference pages. Remember to include the sources you may have referred to in the paper, but didn't actually use in writing your paper. Though discussed earlier under "Citations" it bears repeating again. If, during writing, your sources make reference to someone's study or works, but you don't use that author's study or writings you must either not refer to that author or you must cite the reference page that will supply needed bibliographic information.

Typing and writing instructions, provided later, will guide you in the final preparations of the reference page. Also, there is a guide for writing bibliographic information for sources other than books, periodicals, and encyclopedias.

On the next two pages there are examples from research papers of properly written reference pages. Note the difference between scientific and A-D systems for listing sources.

Literature Cited

Graves, Donald; Lou, Siguan. "Decomposition of Aspartame Caused by Heat in Acidified and Dried State". Jour. Of Agricultural Food Chemistry. Vol. 35: 439-442, Feb. 1987.

Hayakawa, Kazuichi; Schilopp, Tanya; Wong, Osborne. "Determination of Asartic Acid, Phenylalnine, and Aspartylphenylalanine in Aspartame". Jour. Of Agricultural Food Chemistry. Vol. 38: 1256-1260, April 1990.

Homler, Barry. "Aspartame Stability". Food Engineering. Vol. 5: 127-28, May 1984.

Homler, Barry. "Properties and Stability of Aspartame". Food Technology. Vol. 38: 50-55, Jan. 1988.

Stamp, Jeff; LaBuza, Theodore. "An Ion Pair HPLC Method for the Determinetion of Aspartame and its Decomposition Products". Jour. Of Food Science. Vol. 54(4): 1043-46, April 1989.

Tsang, Wing Sum; Clarke, Margaret; Parrish, Fredrick. "HPLC Methods for Determination of Aspartame's Decomposition Products". Jour. Of Agricultural Food Science. Vol. 33(4): 734-738, April 1985.

Tsoubeli, Menexia; LaBuza, Theodore. "Accelerated Kinetic Study of Aspartame Degradation in the Neutral pH Range." Jour. Of Food Science. Vol. 56(6): 1671-75, June 1991.

Figure 8.1. A-D Reference Page

References

1. Charley, Richard J. Water, Earth, and Man: Synthesis of Hydrology, Geomorphology, and Socio-economic Geography. Methuen and Co. Bungay, Suffolk UK, 1969.

2. Groudwater: Saving the Unseen Resources. Final Report of the National Groundwater Policy Forum by The Conservation Foundation, Washington DC, 1987.

3. Price, Michael. Introducing Groundwater. George Allan and Unwin, London UK, 1985.

4. Canter, L.W.; Knox, R.C.; Fairchild, D. Groundwater Quality Protection. Lewis Pub, Inc., Chelsea, Mich, 1988.

5. Quayle, O.R. "The Parachors of Organic Compounds." Chemical Reviews. Vol. 53: 439-585.

6. Moore, J.W.; Ramamoorthy, S. Organic Chemicals in Natural Waters. Springer-Verlag Pub., New York, NY, 1984.

7. Weast, R.C. CRC Handbook of Chemistry and Physics. 54th Ed. CRC Press, Cleveland, OH, 1974.

8. Leo, A.Cc. Hansch; Elkins, D. "Partition Coefficients and Their Uses." Chemical Review. Vol. 71: 525-616.

9. Garbarini, Doug R.; Lion, Leonard W. "Influence of the Nature of Soil Organics on Sorption of Toluene and TCE." Environmental Science and Tech. Vol. 20: 1263-1269, 1986.

10. Gschwend, Philip. "On Consistancy of Sediment - Water Partition Coeffecients of Hydrophobic Organic Pollutants." Environmental Science and Tech. Vol. 19: 90-96, 1985.

11. Stauffer, Thomas B.; MacIntyre, Williams G. "Sorption of Non-polar Organic Chemicals on Low-Carbon-Content Aquifer Materials." Environmental Toxiology and Chemistry. Vol. 8: 845-852, 1989.

Figure 8.2. Scientific Reference Sheet

Chapter 9

THE FINISHED PRODUCT - FINAL ASSEMBLY

Many teachers, particularly at the high school and college levels, will not accept handwritten papers. Even if they will, a typed one always makes a better impression. Following are some guidelines for typing your paper.

Typing the Paper

Read through these instructions carefully before beginning. If something is not clear, ask the instructor to clarify it. Photocopy everything.

Preliminaries

1. Use standard (8.5x11)size white typing paper. If using a pin-feed printer with a word processor, remove the margin holes when completed.
2. Type on one side only.
3. Errors may be erased or corrected with "white-out."

Title page, table of contents, and outline

(If you are using a word processor which has default styles for these pages, get approval from your teacher. Otherwise, follow the guides below.)

1. Arrange the following information neatly on the page:
   - A. Title centered between left and right margins, 20 lines from the top of the paper. (See examples in the Appendix.)
   - B. Your name centered 10 lines below the last line of title
   - C. The date centered 5 lines below your name

2. The table of contents page should list the following by page number:
   A. Outline
   B. Title of research paper - Page 1
   C. References page - Page ____ (You will have to supply the page number.)
3. At the top of the Table of Contents page center the words "Table of Contents" 7 lines from the top of the paper. Triple-space each entry.
4. The outline page should have the word "Outline" centered 7 lines from the top of the paper.
5. Double- space the outline.

The report

1. Double-space the text of the research paper.
2. Use 1 inch (2.0 cm) margins on all sides of all pages except the first page.
3. Leave a 9-space margin on the top of the first page. DO NOT type the title on this page.
4. Number every page of the paper, except the first page. The page number should be an Arabic numeral typed in the center of the page on the 5th line with the text beginning 3 spaces beneath the number.

The reference page

1. Number the reference page in the same fashion as the text.
2. Type one of the following titles 3 spaces below the number: References Cited, Literature Cited, or References. Center the title at the top of the page.
3. Leave 1 inch margins on all other sides. Begin the first entry 3 spaces below the title of the page.

4. Single space the information for each entry. Remember to indent 3 to 6 spaces after the first line. Number the entries as they correspond to the source number in the citation. The A-D system alphabetizes the entry by last name, omitting numerals. (See Figure 7.1.)
5. Double-space each separate entry. (Refer to Figure 7.1 and 7.2)
6. Some word processor programs have default styles for reference pages. Be sure to get approval before using one of these.

Assembling the paper

1. Arrange the paper in the following order: title page, table of contents, outline, report (including diagrams, pictures, etc.), reference page, and a grading page. The grading page should have the words "Grading Page" typed 7 lines from the top of the paper.
2. Submit final paper in a clean, wrinkle-free, 3-prong report folder with a copy of the last rough draft in the back pocket. Photocopy everything.

Eye-catching report jackets are usually welcome. Sometimes an illustrated front cover grabs the reader's attention before reading the introductory paragraph. Avoid hastily hand written or hand drawn titles and illustrations as they can actually distract the reader. Use an extra photocopied diagram or picture and attach it to the cover with a neatly lettered title.

Be certain the folder is clean, and free of wrinkles, folds, and tears. Punch holes if the research paper is typed, and assemble the paper in the brads before submitting it. Also, place the last rough draft in the back pocket of the folder.

Appendix C features a model research paper to help you visualize your own goal in writing an excellent paper.

Table 9.1.
Helpful Hints for the Use of Inserts

1. Use illustrations whenever giving detailed descriptions, especially if the topic is biological.

2. When possible include data tables to support the facts, but avoid lengthy, meaningless tables.

3. Footnote any diagrams, pictures, tables, etc. as if they were part of the report text.

4. In-text placement of support inserts is the preferred method, but they can be added at the end of the text provided they are clearly referred to in the chapter.

5. When preparing an insert, carefully trim the diagram, table, or picture and glue it to the paper with rubber cement or a glue stick (white glue wrinkles the paper).

6. White-out the original caption and add your own figure number and write a new caption (don't forget the citation).

7. Researve one nice illustration for the jacket of the paper.

8. If time permits, photocopy the pages with glued inserts because many times glued items peel off.

Section III.

The Experimental Research Project

Chapter 10

THE LITERATURE REVIEW AND RESEARCH REPORT

The scientific research paper in the form of a literature review is the beginning step of the experimental science project. The knowledge obtained from studying the literature is necessary to comprehend and intelligently discuss your science project. The objective as a researcher is to become the sole authority and expert in your chosen field.

When discussing science projects, it is important to understand that there are four major aspects to consider:

1. **The research paper**
2. **The experimental investigation**
3. **The project display**
4. **The project presentation**

The research paper aspect is only one part, but it ties into the other three. First, an understanding of the topic aids in comprehending the experimental investigation. The project display itself will reflect and draw from your research background. Finally, speaking intelligently about your chosen topic and being able to answer questions relating to the experimental outcome can make the difference between winning and losing in science fair competition or receiving a top grade on a class project.

It is very important to avoid uttering the three deadliest words during a project presentation:

I DON'T KNOW!!

If, in truth, you must say them, your salvation comes if you know the literature thoroughly enough to be able to point out that no one else does either.

There are many variations in science fair and school requirements, for the documentation to accompany an experimental investigation. Some will require the literature review as discussed in this book to be an entirely separate document with respect to other data. Others will expect the literature review to be incorporated as part of a single report of the investigation. In the latter case, as you will note from your study of scientific journals, it is usually placed at the beginning of the paper as part of the background and introductory information.

If a single paper is required, it will usually include the following divisions:

Abstract
Introduction, including literature review
Experimental methods
Results
Discussion of results

In this format, the references are normally placed at the end of the paper, not at the end of the literature review portion.

Many project books have detailed presentation instructions for presenting experimental work. The style requirements for presentation of methods, results, etc. also vary considerably with different scientific disciplines. For these reasons, they are not included in this book. Most scientific journals carry a section of instructions for authors in at least one issue of each volume. If you follow the requirements of a major journal in your field, you will not be criticized for form.

Some science fairs publish the papers of participants or abstracts of the projects. They will provide explicit directions for meeting the requirements. Be sure to follow them to the letter, as some are related to mechanical requirements for scanned or camera-ready copy.

The remainder of this section will be concerned with the vital topic of choosing a subject for your research, whether it is experimental or a literature review.

Chapter 11

CHOOSING A RESEARCH SUBJECT

Professional scientists and engineers might want to skim quickly over this section because their employer has already chosen the subject for them!

Probably everyone will agree that the single most difficult hurdle in the science project process is choosing a suitable investigation topic. There are volumes of science project books on the market. Begin by searching the local library. Ask for help locating the science-fair project books.

The first step in selecting a topic is to narrow the search to a particular field of study. In most science fairs there are 12 or 13 subject areas: behavioral and social sciences, biochemistry, botany, chemistry, computer, earth and space, engineering, environmental science, mathematics, medicine and health, microbiology, physics, and zoology. Each of the major categories are further narrowed into sub-categories, such as mechanical engineering, chemical engineering, aeronautical engineering, etc.

When searching for a topic or topics, keep in mind the following guidelines:

1. **It is interesting to you.**
2. **It has relevance to today's world (real life application).**
3. **It is a specific enough topic with enough material written about it.**
4. **It is experimental in nature (it answers a specific question).**
5. **It is challenging, but not overwhelming.**

Don't be afraid to tackle a difficult category or topic. The whole point of the research aspect is to familiarize yourself with the subject chosen. Be prepared with three or four topics (questions) or subjects just in case some are rejected by the instructor or someone has already received approval for a similar topic.

The question always arises as to where you can find topic ideas. Science project books have already been mentioned, but these aren't the only source for ideas. Below are some other places to search.

* **General science textbooks**
* **High school or college laboratory manuals**
* **College psychology textbooks (if you choose social sciences)**
* **Scientific journals (*Scientific American* and *Jour. Of Chemical Education* are excellent sources.)**
* ***International Science and Engineering Fair abstracts* (published yearly; contains 100's of projects)**
* **Regional and State science fairs from previous years**
* **Professional people such as medical doctors, college professors, psychologists, and engineers - talk to them**
* **If worse comes to worst, YOUR INSTRUCTOR**

Avoid oversimplified, overworked topics. These types of projects are either too easy or they appear in every science fair in multiple copies. Your instructor reserves the right to make the final judgement on appropriateness of topic.

Examples of oversimplified and overworked project ideas might include:

- **volcanoes**
- **consumer products testing (which works best??)**
- **solar systems**
- **Acid rain and plants**
- **electric motors**
- **airfoils and wing shapes**

- **magnetism (electromagnets)**
- **rock and soil collections**
- **pendulums**
- **caffeine experiments**
- **plants and colored lights**
- **music and moods or emotions**
- **stream erosion**
- **respiration experiments**
- **probability projects (math)**
- **some types of right-left brain project**

This is not an exhaustive list of overdone topic choices and some of these subjects could even be used if you add a new "twist" or approach to the subject from a fresh perspective. Certainly, don't be afraid to ask your instructor for topic suggestions and modifications. Above all, have your instructor's blessing before starting.

Keep in mind that the subject you choose must lend itself to scientific experimentation, such as a chemical analysis of a rock. Obviously volcanoes and rock collections are demonstration-type projects and would make poor choices for experiments.

A word about two-year projects: Projects sometimes can be continued for several years. Many projects at State and International science fairs are three and four year projects. If you feel your project could continue beyond one year, you must improve the experimental design and do further literature research using new and more advanced references. Simply rewriting your old research paper and repeating your project is not sufficient. You should obtain prior approval from your instructor for second year projects.

Finally, beware of plagiarizing someone else's old project. It is not appropriate to take someone else's data from a previously exhibited project and claim it as your own. Also, it is inappropriate to repeat a project you exhibited from a previous year and present it as new or original work. However, it is alright to get an idea from a previous year's project as long as it is your original work. If in doubt, check with your instructor.

After finding suitable topic ideas, submit the list to your instructor for final approval. Write your full name and date on a full sheet of notebook paper along with the topic choices. Your instructor will "O.K." the best idea. If there is someone else who wants to do a similar project, the person who first submits the idea will be given first priority.

After the topic has been approved, it is a good idea to do some preliminary literature searching to make sure there is enough accessible material published about your topic. If most of the information is found only in scientific journals, begin planning how to obtain the necessary articles. If your school or public library doesn't carry the journal, check with nearby college and university libraries.

Section IV.

Evaluation and Grading

Chapter 12

MIDDLE SCHOOL/JR. HIGH RESEARCH PAPER CRITERIA

The very backbone of a good science project is the research paper. General requirements for the Jr. High project research paper are as follows:

Rough drafts: minimum of 1200-1400 words (not including footnotes)
Bibliography cards: min. of 6 different sources
Outlines
Note cards: min. of 45
Final draft: 1000-1200 words (not including footnotes)

Cited Source Requirements:

1. **A minimum of 6 different sources, including:**
   - A. Books
   - B. Science magazines or journals (at least one is required)
   - C. One encyclopedia, copyrighted since 1998
   - D. Other sources (see below)
2. **A Word Concerning Books**

   You may use as many books as you need and there is no minimum number; try to find books that contain current information. Also try to avoid "pop" science books that provide only brief, general information or do not document their own sources. College text books provide good information and usually contain a reference section and bibliography.

3. **A Word Concerning Encyclopedias**

Any well known general encyclopedia will meet the source requirements, but science encyclopedias are preferred. You have the option to substitute other books and magazine articles for the encyclopedia. Also be aware that several volumes of the same encyclopedia will count only as one source.

4. **A Word Concerning Magazine and Journal Articles**

The magazine source requirement must come from a reputable science magazine or journal. Some magazines which are not acceptable sources might include: *Reader's Digest, Time, Newsweek, Good Housekeeping, McCall's,* and *Redbook.* However, they are valuable as a source of ideas for searching the scientific literature. If you found a magazine reference using the Periodical Index or InfoTrack check with your teacher before using the article, as often these sources have very limited scientific merit. Newspaper articles are also not acceptable scientific sources.

5. **About Other Sources**

The very minimum requirement of sources is six. However, these six sources need not be only printed sources. For instance, videos, TV programs (of scientific merit), tapes, and interviews are acceptable forms of sources provided they are properly documented (cited with entry in bibliography).

Literature Search

The local public library and university libraries have all the books and magazines you could use. However, if you are having difficulty locating a magazine or journal article, the public library has two excellent periodical indexes for locating articles:

1. ***The General Science Index*: Lists by topic thousands of article titles and references**

2. ***The Social Science Index*: Similar in format to the *GSI*, but is restricted to articles relating to psychology, animal behavior, and human development**

Should you find a book the public library doesn't have check with the Interlibrary loan system at the information desk. Through Interlibrary loan you can order books from other library systems. Allow yourself 2-3 weeks for delivery time. If you find an excellent journal article but its source is located at a different local college library, write the full reference on a piece of paper and perhaps your teacher can obtain it. Many community college libraries also have good sources and reference sections. Photocopy the entire article along with its own bibliography. Be sure to write down the BIBLIOGRAPHIC information on the photocopies!!! You will need to provide money for photocopies.

Written Graded Requirements

1. A written outline at the onset of your research paper - This should contain 3 to 4 major points with 2 to 4 subpoints. It can be modified and changed up to three weeks before the first rough draft is due. Keep your main points and subpoints brief and avoid long rambling sentences. Don't be too general or vague in your outline, but on the other hand don't be too excessive. One or two pages should be the maximum length.

2. At least six bibliography cards -You may add more cards as you research.

3. At least 45 note cards, from your sources - They must correspond to your research paper outline.

4. At least one penciled rough draft 1200 to 1400 words containing citations corresponding to your minimum 6 sources - A penciled final outline and bibliography are also included.

5. A final ink or typed draft, 1000-1200 words containing the following: title page, table of contents, outline, paper to include footnotes, diagrams, pictures, tables, bibliography, and grading page

The paper must be presented in a clean, unused 3-brad pocket folder containing the most recent rough draft. The folder can be theme decorated.

Final word: If you don't have a library card - get one. Always refer to your research paper calendar and note any changes along the way.

Chapter 13

HIGH SCHOOL/INTRODUCTORY COLLEGE CRITERIA

The key to an award winning science project is good background research. Through research you become the expert in your field of study. This expertise is important when discussing your project with science fair judges and the general public. The first step to being an expert is to search and digest important information about your topic. The research paper provides the opportunity to see what other researchers have found concerning your project topic. When you submit your final draft, you should be able to stand and speak confidently about your topic.

General Requirements

- 1300-1600 word rough draft with footnotes, outline, and bibliography in pencil
- 1200-1400 word final draft with outline, footnotes, bibliography, etc. typed
- Cited sources: a minimum of eight (including two magazine articles)

Source requirements

Book requirement: there is no minimum number of books. You may substitute magazine or journal articles for books.

Periodicals: a minimum of four magazine or journal articles required.

Optional source: encyclopedia. You may substitute a book or periodical source for the encyclopedia. Only one encyclopedia is permitted with some restrictions (see guidelines).

Other sources: tapes, videos, interviews are acceptable but must be documented properly.

Source Guidelines and Restrictions

Books: There are no restrictions except to use books with more current information. Books copyrighted before 1980 are probably not current.

Periodicals: Periodicals are probably the most important and most current information available. Therefore, its very important to obtain articles form professional scientific magazines and journals. Magazines of questionable scientific merit are not permitted.

Professional scientific periodicals with reputable scientific merit might include the following:

American Biology Teacher
American Journal of Physics
Child Development
Computer and Control Abstracts
Energy Information Abstracts Annual
Environmental Periodicals Bibliography
Environmental Science and Technology
International Aerospace Abstracts
International Bibliography
Journal of AmericanMedical Association
Journal of American Psychology
Journal of Chemical Education
Nature
Oceanic Abstracts
Physics Abstracts

Pollution Abstracts
Science
Scientific American

Encyclopedias: Use general encyclopedias for outline ideas only. If you choose to exercise your option to use an encyclopedia, use scientific encyclopedias found in reference sections of the public library or local college and university libraries. Encyclopedias having good scientific merit include the following:

Encyclopedia of Chemical Technology
Grzimeks Animal Life Encyclopedia
McGraw-Hill Encyclopedia of Science **(includes bibliographies)**
Plants and Earth Science

Source Locations and Locators

The public library system has many useful volumes of good scientific merit. However; they carry few professional journals. Most Community College and University libraries have a wide periodical circulation with most titles going back to the mid-1970's. The public library has two excellent magazine indexes: ***The General Science Index*** and ***The Social Science Index.***

In addition to the above indexes, there are many other very useful indexes as described on pages 14-17.

Beware of the InfoTrack system in the public library. Most of the articles referenced there are of questionable scientific merit. Check with your teacher before using an article from InfoTrack.

If you are not a student, most college libraries will not permit you to check out books, but you can photocopy (p/c) pages for about ten cents a copy. If you find a book you need, use the Interlibrary system at the public library. Through the Interlibrary loan system you can order any book in circulation from anywhere in the U.S. Allow at least 2-3 weeks for delivery.

A very important point to remember whenever you p/c something is to get all the BIBLIOGRAPHY information copied onto the p/c.

Written requirements

1. Research outline of at least 3-4 main points and sub-points - Keep the points brief and avoid pronouns.
2. At least 8 bibliography cards - Two must be scientific magazines.
3. A minimum of 60 note cards corresponding to the sources and outline
4. At least one penciled rough draft of 1300-1600 words, double-spaced, to include outline, footnotes and bibliography
5. A typed final draft 1200-1400 words - The draft must include: title page, outline (in final form), typed and footnoted report (include diagrams, pictures and tables), bibliography, and grading page.
6. Paper must be presented in a new, clean 3-brad pocket folder which will contain the latest rough draft in the front pocket. Its not a bad idea to p/c your final draft in case something gets lost. Diagrams, pictures, tables, and charts must be footnoted just like any source used and included in the final bibliography.

Appendix A

Grading And Proofreading Notations

On the next two pages are some examples of the common correction notations you may find written on the first draft. There are many others which your teacher may use. They are all written on the draft to draw attention to a problem. Be sure to consult this list and other symbols you might add while re-writing and correcting the paper.

(Word) ?	The word(s) circled is not understandable or hard to read
(Word) def	term circled must be defined or explained briefly
(Wrod) sp	circled word is misspelled-check the dictionary for spelling
~~Word~~	omit term or phrase from text of paper
???	term or sentence doesn't make sense or has an unclear meaning
w/o	write out the word or phrase - don't use "" marks
⋀	insert word or phrase
word the	transpose word or phrase (transpose means change the order)
Caps	use capital letters or capitalize the term
¶	needs a paragraph break, new thought

Intro ¶	Paper needs introductory paragraph
conclusion ¶	paper needs summary paragraph
(Source)	a footnote is needed at the end of last sentence
Dia	diagram is needed in text of final draft - this is not an option and therefore the final draft grade will be lowered
biblio.?	where is the bibliography or literature cited page?
inc	Incomplete sentence or thought - re-write sentence
 ➡	indent where arrow points
 ⁀‿	close up
	delete
⊙	period is needed
#	space is needed

Appendix B

Sample Evaluation Forms

The following evaluation forms are those used by the author with his students. Some teachers may wish to use them as shown; others will want to modify them for their particular circumstances. Some large schools have standard forms used by all teachers in the science department. Even if the form is not used "as is," it will provide a handy checklist for most students.

Professional scientists and engineers who are reviewing this book may find the forms a useful guide to make certain everything is in place before submitting a research report. Research managers often react to papers in much the same way a teacher would.

Research Paper Process Record

Student Name					
Source Cards					
outline 1					
outline 2					
source 1					
source 2					
source 3					
source 4					
source 5					
source 6					
source 7					
source 8					
source 9					
source 10					
Final outline					
Introduction					
Reference page					
1st draft					
2nd draft					
Total points					
bonus points					
Final Tally					

Item of Paper	Points if Missing	Points for Errors
Title Page	**5**	**1-3 if incorrect**
Table of contents	**5**	**1 if incorrect**
Outline	**10**	**1-3 if incorrect**
Intro Paragraph	**5**	**2 if "weak"**
Footnotes/citations	**10/source** **5/diagram**	**1 if incorrect**
Grammar that Pronouns Other offenses	 **2pts** **2pts** **1/offense**	
Diagrams	**10 if told to include** **5 if needed more**	
Concluding paragraphs	**5 if missing**	**2pts if "weak"**
Reference page	**15 if missing**	
Periodicals	**10 pts. no periodicals**	
Documented	**5/source if cited but not referenced**	
Format	**5 for indentation**	**2 if not equally spaced**
Grading page	**3 if missing**	
Other points early extra sources	 **+5 for process** **+5 for 9-10 sources** **+10 for more than 10**	
Content excellent 94-100 very good 88-93 good 80-87 fair 76-79 poor 68-75	**Process** source notes missing sources outline biblio. Cards final draft	**Points** 10 if under min. 3 per source 10 if under min. 5 if not turned in 5 if late

Below is a representative grading sheet used in evaluating student research papers. It can be adapted to individual needs for grading. With some changes it could also be implemented as a "check-off" sheet by the students.

Name ____________________ Grade____ Section_________
Title ____

Structure
Title Page ____
Table of Contents ____
Outline ____

Body of Paper
Introduction ____
Citations ____
(Check-off) ____

1	2	3	4	5	6	7	8	9	10	others
___	___	___	___	___	___	___	___	___	___	_____

Grammar/Lang.
Wording/use of slang ____
Sentence structure ____
Use of pronouns ____
Clear paragraphs ____
Following outlines ____
Diagrams ____
Tables & graphs ____
Conclusions ____
Reference page ____
Books ____
Periodicals ____
Form ____
Grading page ____
Other notations ____

Bonus Points
Extra sources ____
Extra illustrations ____
Folder ____
Early presentation ____

Finalizing the grade. The three areas to consider:
Process - turning things in on time.
Structure - meeting the basic requirements.
Content - scientific accuracy.

Structure Points Worksheet
Points deducted ____
Bonus points ____
Final tally (enter below) ____

Grading Breakdown
Process ____
Structure ____
Content ____
Final average ____

Grade Level	**7th & 8th**	**9th & 10th**	**11th & 12th**
Rough Draft	Two: 1200 to 1400 words	Two: 1300 to 1500 words	Two: 1500 to 1700 words
Biblio. Cards	Six: 5 books 1 periodical	Eight: 6 books 2 periodicals	Ten: 6 books 4 periodicals
Outlines	Three: 2 roughs 1 final	2 roughs 1 final 4-5 point	Four: 3 roughs 1 final 5-7 point
Note Cards	40-45	50-60	60-75
Final Draft	one: 1000 to 1200 words (typing opt.)	One: 1200 to 1400 words (typing preferred)	Typed: 1400 to 1600 words

Appendix C
Writing Exercises

1. Look up the following words in a thesaurus. Locate at least two synonyms for each to convey a more scientific meaning.

make	**deny (negation)**
difference	**useless**
concern	**show (as to display)**
necessary (adjective)	**take part**
fix	**reach (noun and verb)**
many	**end**

2. Rewrite the following introductory paragraph to give it more life. Correct any grammatical errors and eliminate use of pronouns or unnecessary "verbiage". Use the outline on page 11 for help.

   The research report I'm going to tell about is about sunspots. It will tell about how they form. And it will show a lot about astronomers who study the sun. Then it will talk about sunspot cycles and how they work. Then the report will end talking about sunspot rotation. (49 words)

3. Rewrite the following introductory paragraph. Correct grammar, spelling, and substitute more challenging words wherever possible (use a thesaurus). Rewrite to eliminate personal pronouns and "verbiage" and reduce the overall length of the paragraph.

   A lot of information is written about insects, but have you ever studied one insect in particular? This report will do that. First I will talk about metamorhosis. Then it will deal with the misquito. Included in my report is the life cycle and behavior of it. (Including all the stages of growth.) After that, I'll spend a little time dealing with its enveronmental stress factors such as acidic water. (69 words)

4. Use the "Mosquito Outline" in Chapter 1 to write an intelligent introductory paragraph. Use good writing techniques and avoid the writing errors mentioned in Table 5. Have your thesaurus and dictionary handy to use the best words to convey the meaning of the topic.

5. Use your own research outline, write an introductory paragraph. Use a thesaurus and Table 5 as help. Try to keep the length to less than 70 words. If time permits, set your paragraph aside for several days and then rewrite it or have a friend read the paragraph to get a "second opinion" and then rewrite it.

6. Look up the term "plagiarism" in the dictionary. Why would copying a sentence or paragraph from a published source be unwise? If you wanted to use a sentence from a published source what would be your writing options? (See the discussion "Documentation and Footnoting" in Chapter 2 for help.)

7. Describe briefly the difference between "scientific citations" and the "APA citation" methods.

8. Use the bibliography cards from Chapter 1 exercises to write a reference page. Follow the guidelines appropriate for the "scientific citation" method.[1]

9. Use the following outline on the subject of lipids to write an intelligent introductory paragraph. Use a thesuarus for word selection and review the most common writing errors found in Table 5 to achieve your goal. Keep the word count to under 70.

Topic: Lipids

- **I. Types, Purposes, and Function of Lipids**
  - **A. Lipid Classification**
    1. **Fats and oils**
    2. **Phosphollipids**
    3. **Steroid**
  - **B. Function of Lipids in Biosystems**
- **II. Structures and Properties of Lipids**
  - **A. Distinguishing Functional Groups**
    1. **Carboxylic acid group**
    2. **Nonpolar carbon chain**
  - **B. Properties and Structural Features**
    1. **Solubility in water**
    2. **Polarity**
    3. **Saturation and unsaturation**
- **III. The Role of Lipids In Cellular Membranes**
  - **A. Composition of Cell Membranes**
    1. **Lipid bilayers**
    2. **The fluid mosaic model**
  - **B. Function of Cell Membranes**
    1. **Mechanical barriers**
    2. **Controlling the passage of molecules and ions**
    3. **Providing structural support for proteins**

10. Rewrite the following paragraph using fewer words, better sentence structure, and more scientific terms. Also correct any other problems such as spelling, grammatical errors, and use of personal pronouns. [2]

    The 3rd factor, pH, is kind of important to aspartame being stable. As mentioned in chapter 7 a lot of moist or liquid food products is found in the pH range of 3.0 to 5.0 wich is the stability range of it. Ice cream, for instance shows temperature and pH interaction but is well beyond aspartame's stability range showing that if you keep it cold it will have a slower decomposition rate meaning aspartame won't go away as much as if it were warmer. (81 words)

What evidence in the above paragraph suggests this student plagiarized someone's writing? What should have appeared at the end of this paragraph?

11. Use the bibliography cards from your own research paper to write a practice Reference page. Refer to the section in Chapter 2, titled "The Reference and Further Reading Page" for help.

Instructor's Notes: [1] You may wish to have students do both scientific and the APA style reference page.
[2] You may wish to go over this exercise with the class together pointing out problems and have students correct them as you proceed. Doing this will give opportunities to review writing style, sentence structure, proper grammar, and footnoting.

Appendix D
Aspartame: Determination and Detection of Decomposition Products

Publishers note:
The original paper used here was much longer with many more charts and graphs. Some of these have been deleted to save space and make the style characteristics easier to follow.

Research Outline

I. Introduction

II. Chemical Description of Aspartame
- **A. Composition of Aspartame**
- **B. Decomposition of Aspartame**
- **C. Products of Decomposition**
  - *1. L-aspartyl -L-phenylalanine*
  - *2. diketopiperazine*

III. Aspartame's Stability and Kinetics
- **A. Factors Affecting Stability**
  - *1. Time*
  - *2. Temperature range*
  - *3. pH range*
- **B. Mechanisms of Decomposition of Aspartame**

IV. Select Studies on Decomposition Products
- **A. Tsang, Clark, and Parrish (1985)**
- **B. Stamps and LaBuza (1989)**
- **C. Hayakawa, Schilpp, and Wong (1990)**

(The first page of text has different margins than other pages. See Appen. D)

The 1982 approval by the FDA for general use of the artificial sweetener aspartame created quite a stir among consumers. Here, at last, was an artificial sweetener having less than 1% of sugar's calories and a taste nearly indistinguishable from sugar's. This research paper will describe some of aspartame's properties, its sustainability, and kinetics. It will also highlight studies pertaining to its decomposition products and quantitative techniques in determining those products. (*Introductory paragraph See pgs. 20-22, Fig. 9)*

Aspartame, L-aspartyl-L-phenylalanine methyl ester (APM), is a dipeptide made up of two amino acids: L-aspartic acid and L-phenylalanine methyl ester. *(IIA from Outline)* When taken into the body they are metabolized in a similar manner as proteins eaten every day. It is intensely sweet - about 200 times sweeter than sugar. (1,127)

Unfortunately, in the presence of moisture, certain pH conditions, and elevated temperatures, the ester and amine bonds are subject to hydrolysis. Generally, the ester bond is broken first, in case of aspartame the alcohol is replaced by the amino acid group of aspartic acid creating cyclic diketopiperine. *(IIC from Outline)* The degradation products of APM are L-aspartyl phenylalanine (AP) and 2,5 disubstituted *diketopiperazine* (DKP). This comes about by aminolysis of the methyl ester linkage. (1,128) The dipeptide aspartyl phenylalanine can be produced by either ring opening of DKP or directly by hydrolysis of the methyl ester. The final step is hydrolysis of dipeptide into amino acids, none of which are themselves sweet. (2,1256) *(Citation format. See pgs. 24-25, and figure 10-12)* The general reaction appears in Figure 1. (2,157)*(Diagram citation See pg. 24.)*

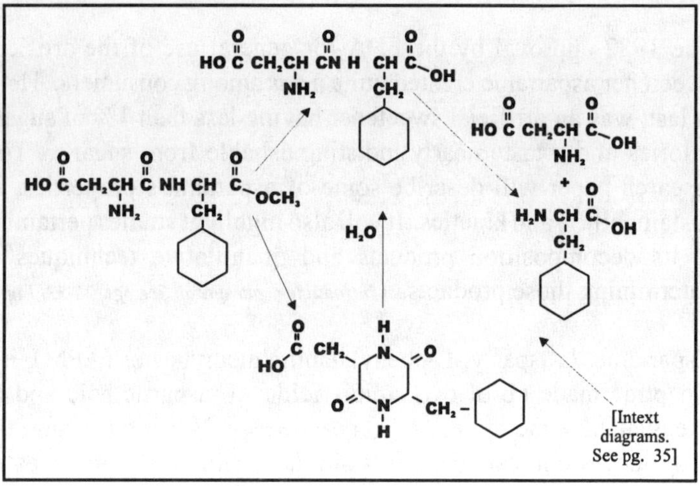

[Intext diagrams. See pg. 35]

Figure 1

The stability of aspartame in solution (where used as a sweetener in soft drinks or dairy beverages) is a function of three primary factors: [time, temperature, and pH]. Perceptible sweetness is reduced as the per cent of undecomposed aspartame decreases. This is especially true for temperature increase for a given time period. Through experimentation, the decomposition follows 1st order kinetics. ***(IIIA from Outline)***

The relations between pH, and the other factors are important to aspartame's stability. Most moist or liquid food products exist in an acid range of pH 3.0 to 5.0 which happens to be the stability range of aspartame. At 25° C, aspartames half-life peaks at around pH 4.3. Similar results occur at 40 and 55° C. However, at 80° C, there is a stability shift to the pH 6-7 range. Thus, decomposition over a 24 hour period is very slight as long as the pH is between 3.0 and 4.0. Figure 2 shows stability at various pH ranges. (3,52) ***(IIIB from Outline)***

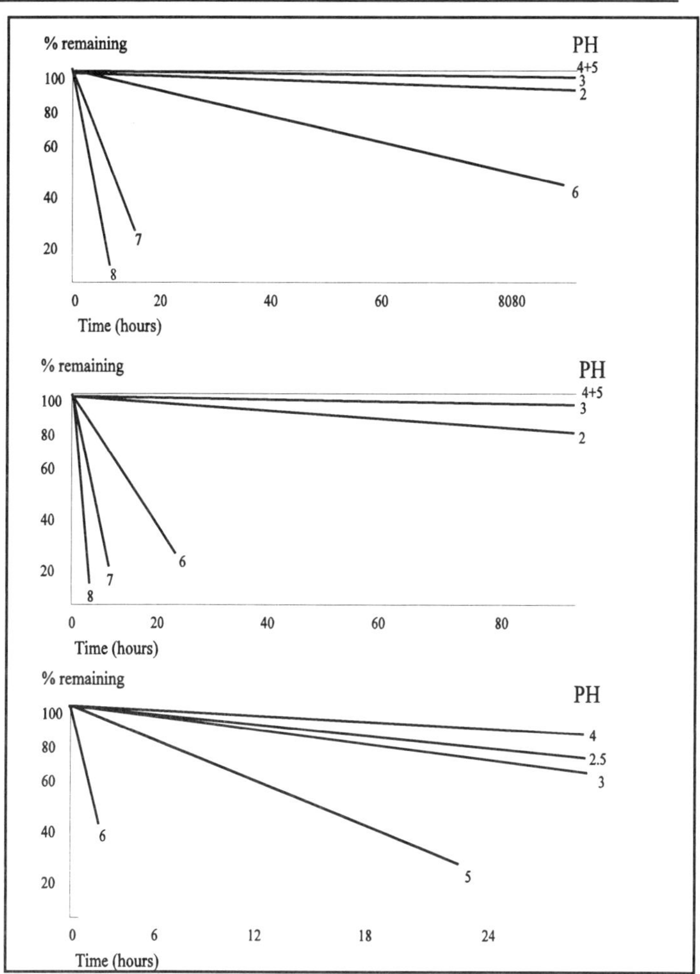

% remaining
PH
100
80
60
40
20
4+5
3
2
6
7
8
0
20
40
60
8080
Time (hours)
% remaining
PH
100
80
60
40
20
4+5
3
2
6
7
8
0
20
40
60
80
Time (hours)
% remaining
PH
100
80
60
40
20
4
2.5
3
6
5
0
6
12
18
24
Time (hours)

Figure 2.

Ice cream illustrates temperature and pH interaction. It has a pH range of 6.5 to 7.0, well outside of aspartame's stability range, but since it is kept in temperatures well below 0° C, the reaction rate is reduced. The semilog plot of percentage of remaining aspartame verses time is a straight line with a slope of K_{obs}. (4,1672) Tables 1 and 2 summarize rate constants for several conditions studied by Tsoubeli and LaBuza in 1991. (4,1673) *(IIIC)*

Table 1

Rate consists (=95% confidence limits) for aspartame degradation, effects of acidity and temperature

System		Rate constants (hr^{-1})			
		70 °C	80 °C	90 °C	100 °C
M	pH	(r^2)	(r^2)	(r^2)	(r^2)
0.01	7.0	1.20=0.20 (0.98)	2.40=0.14 (0.99)	3.80=0.32 (0.99)	7.50=1.03 (0.98)
0.01	6.5	0.16=0.04 (0.98)	0.36=0.14 (0.96)	1.10=0.01 (0.99)	1.40=0.22 (0.96)
0.01	6.0	0.01=0.002 (0.93)	0.03=0.001 (0.93)	0.07=0.01 (0.97)	0.15=0.03 (0.94)
0.05	7.0	3.10=0.20 (0.99)	4.80=1.00 (0.95)	11.20=2.90 (0.94)	20.70=6.60 (0.91)
0.05	6.5	1.0=0.05 (0.99)	2.10=0.20 (0.99)	4.60=0.90 (0.95)	8.90=1.47 (0.97)
0.01	7.0	5.7=0.90 (0.97)	9.30=1.30 (0.98)	16.60=5.6 (0.89)	28.60=10.13 (0.96)
0.01	6.5	1.95=0.08 (0.99)	4.20=0.70 (0.97)	7.10=1.00 (0.97)	12.20=2.50 (0.95)
0.01	6.0	0.41=0.02 (0.99)	1.04=0.06 (0.99)	2.30=0.12 (0.99)	5.90=0.90 (0.97)

Table 2

Half life for aspartame degradation as affected by acidity and temperature with (rate increase factoer as compared to lowest pH tested)

System		Half life (min)			
M	pH	70 °C	80 °C	90 °C	100 °C
0.01	7.0	35 (112)	17 (68)	11 (38)	5.5 (56)
0.01	6.5	208 (15.7)	115 (12)	38 (14.5)	30 (5)
0.01	6.0	4158	1386	594	278
0.05	7.0	13 (3.5)	9 (2.1)	3.7 (2.7)	2 (2.7)
0.05	6.5	42	20	9	5
0.1	7.0	7 (14.6)	5 (8.4)	2.5 (9)	1.5 (7)
0.1	6.5	22 (4.3)	10 (4.2)	6 (3.6)	3.4 (1.9)
0.1	6.0	104	40	18	7

In a study of dried state decomposition, aspartame can dehydrate to form anhydride containing species when heated. The mechanism for the formation of the anhydride is illustrated in Figure 3. (5,439) *(Diagram citation. Fig. 12)*

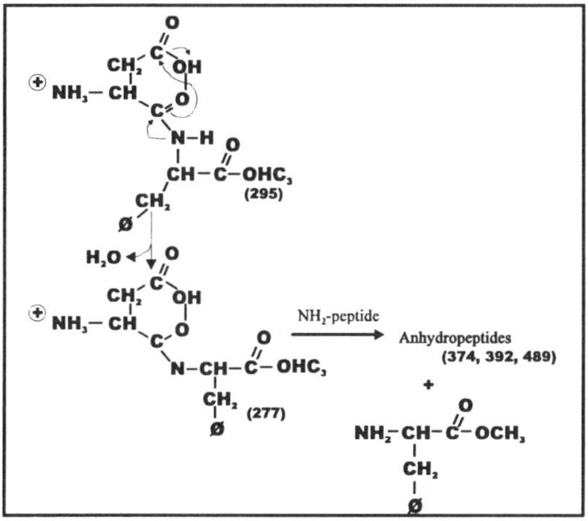

Figure 3.

Aspartame's instability under acidified conditions is probably due to the protonation of the B-carboxyl group. Without protonation, the O- of the carboxylate is a poor leaving group which could explain why the cyclization, shown in Figure 3, is not seen under neutral conditions, pH 7.0. (5,441) ***(IIIC from Outline)***

A variety of methods have been investigated and numerous studies conducted in the area of detection and identification of aspartame and its decomposition products. Some of the methods include thin layer chromatography (Daniels, 1984; Sherman, 1985); high performance liquid chromatography (Schertz, 1983; Prudel, 1986; Stamp and LaBuza, 1989); and IR spectrometry (Chess and Gerson, 1986). Aspartame decomposition follows acid-base catalyst in solution form first DKP (the major decomposition product) followed by base catalyzed hydrolysis of the methyl ester with loss of methanol (Figure 2). ***(Further reading. See pg ?)***

As stated in the introduction to this paper, one of the main objectives is to briefly investigate research experiments representative of separation, detection, and quantification of aspartame's decomposition products. Three studies will be highlighted.

Tsang, Clark, and Parrish, 1985.

In 1985, researchers at Sugar Processing Research, Inc., New Orleans, Louisiana published their findings in the Journal of Agricultural Food Science. ***(IVA from Outline)*** Up until 1985, HPLC methods for determining aspartame had been reported but no attempts had been made to identify any of the decomposition products except by Schertz in 1983. Tsang, Clarke, and Parrish, in their 1985 study, investigated the effects of storage on aspartame in soft drinks which were stored for various lengths of time at room temperature (22 +/- 1° C). The soft drinks were analyzed for aspartame, AP, and DKP using an isocratic HPLC procedure.

Their procedure involved several types of soft drinks stored at six and thirty-six month periods. They used a Waters Associates Model 200 LC equipped with a Model 600A pump and an extended wavelength module. The columns were C-18 reverse phase column (3.9mm X 30cm). Four decomposition products and their relative proportions are shown in Table 3. (6,736)

Table 3

Levels of aspartame and its degradation products in soft drinks after prolonged storage (6 and 36 months).

	6 months storage				36 months storage			
	Lme-Lemon No.1	Lime-Lemon No. 2	Diet Cola No.1	Diet Cola No.2	Lime-Lemon No.1	Lime-Lemon No.2	Diet Cola No.1	Diet Cola No.2
Aspartame (APM)								
label claim, µg/mL	300	490	450	550	300	490	450	550
found,µg/mL	170.66	180.55	171.67	155.34	41.15	31.37	18.44	19.70
% of APM claim	56.89	36.85	38.15	28.24	13.72	6.40	4.10	3.58
L-phenylalnine methyl								
ester found, µg/mL	11.05	21.53	21.26	28.62	5.69	8.59	9.50	13.01
APM equiv	18.14	35.35	34.91	46.99	9.34	14.10	15.60	21.36
% of APM claim	6.05	7.21	7.76	8.54	3.11	2.88	3.47	3.88
DKP								
found,µg/mL	45.76	99.60	96.14	135.66	84.79	145.90	127.50	173.28
APM equiv	51.39	111.85	107.97	152.35	95.22	163.85	143.18	194.59
% of APM claim	17.13	22.83	23.99	27.70	31.74	33.44	31.82	35.38
L-aspartylphenylalanine								
found, µg/mL	52.85	102.75	111.61	158.31	93.91	149.06	141.96	189.05
APM equiv	55.49	107.89	117.19	166.23	98.61	156.51	149.06	198.50
% of APM claim	18.50	22.02	26.04	30.22	32.87	31.94	33.12	36.09
L-phenylalanine								
found, µg/mL	6.75	19.70	29.01	42.22	30.55	67.20	74.00	101.27
APM equiv	12.03	35.11	51.70	75.22	54.44	119.75	131.87	180.46
% of APM claim	4.01	7.16	11.49	13.68	18.15	24.44	29.30	32.81
total aspartame								
accounted for, %	102.58	96.07	107.43	108.38	99.59	99.10	101.81	111.74

All samples of soft drinks, except one, contained less than 40% of the label claim for six month aspartame content. Three samples contained less than 10% after thirty-six months. Within four weeks, over 10% of the aspartame had decomposed in most of the test samples. Figure 4 shows a chromagram of a diet cola and lemon-lime soda comparing six and thirty-six month storage results. (6,738)

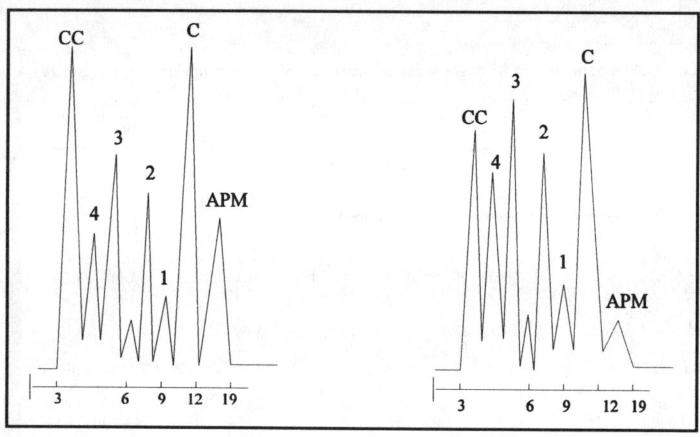

Figure 4.

Stamps and LaBuza, 1989.

In 1989, Stamps and LaBuza (7) researched the retention behavior of aspartame and six decomposition products via ion-pair mobile phase modifiers in HPLC. The objective of their study was to develop a simple isocrate ion-pair reverse phase HPLC procedure for the separation and quantification of aspartame and its decomposition products. The significance of an ion-pair was to slow the effect of pairing ion chain length and mobile phase pH on peak symmetry, resolution, and retention behavior of the substances in question. ***(IVB from Outline)***

Optimum separation of aspartame's decomposition products was obtained by using an isocratic mobile phase of acetonitrile, monosodium phosphate buffer, and 1-heptane adjusted to pH 3. The aqueous components were prepared by dissolving five millimoles of sulfonic acid sodium salt with five millimoles of monosodium phosphate. The isocratic mobile phase was prepared from a mixture of 20/80 percent by volume of acetonitrile and the aqueous component after which the pH was adjusted to 3 utilizing 85% phosphoric acid. The actual flow rate was set to 1.0 mL/min with detection absorbance at 214 nm.

Cola samples were used for analysis after being degassed, sealed in glass ampules, and heated to 80° C for predetermined time intervals. One mL cola samples were diluted in 24 mL of the aqueous portion to then be analyzed by HPLC.

The comparison between the mobile phase with only acetonitrile/monosodium phosphate buffer and the alkyl sulfonic acid can be seen in Figure 5. The chromagram in Figure 6 (7,1043) shows poor resolution of the decomposition products; for example, peaking trails in the last three. The chromogram in Figure 7 (7, 1044) shows effecient seperation. Notice the reverse order of separation between DKP and Phe. ***(IVC from Outline)***

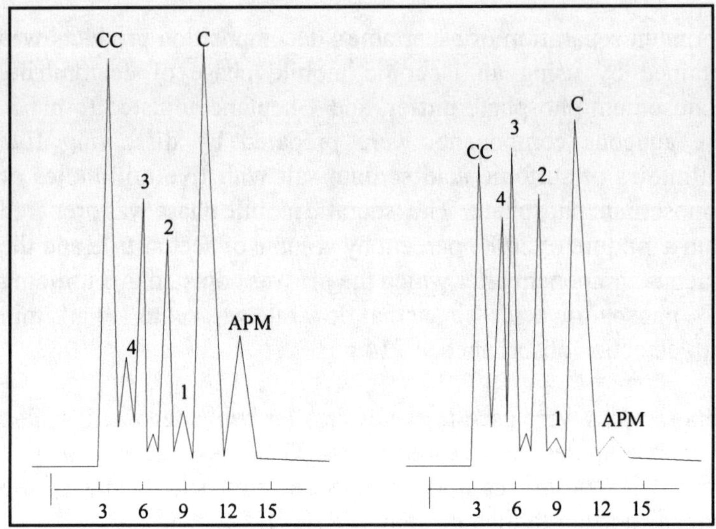

Figure 5.

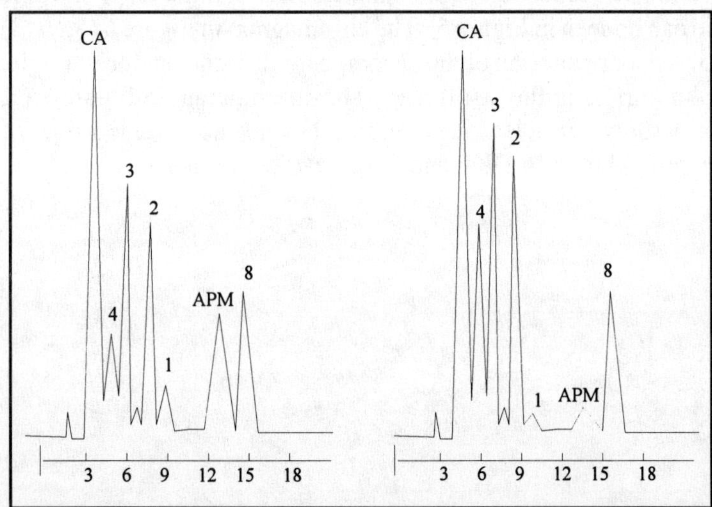

Figure 6.

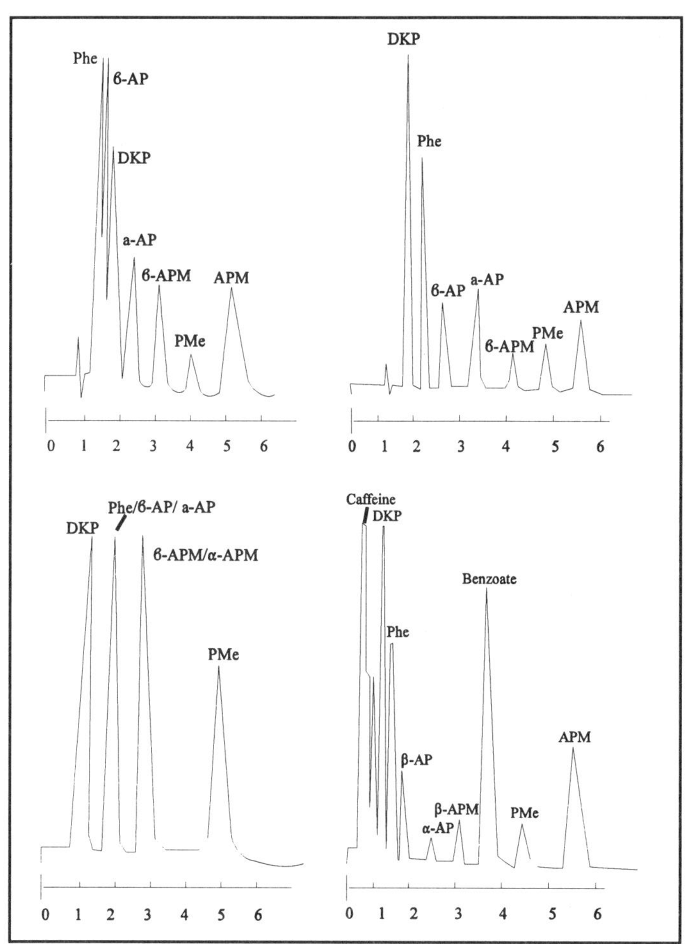

Figure 7.

The study goes on to describe experimentation at varying pH levels, methods for improved peak symmetry, and linearity for all the products analyzed.

Hyakawa, Schilpp, and Wong, 1990.

In 1990, the Journal of Food Chemistry published a research project outlining a method for determining accurately the levels of aspartame and its hydrolysis products. As in previously published research, the chief method of separation was HPLC. In this particular research, however, the levels of Asp and Phe were not determined because neither of these have the properties necessary to quantify their concentrations at the micromolar levels.

The key to this problem lies in some chromographic method which will enhance the absorptivity of the substances in question. The method reported by Hayakawa, Schilpp, and Wong (2) was chemical derivatization, particularly fluorogenic derivatization for primary amines. One such fluorogenic reported reaction involved the reaction of an amine with naphthalene-2,3-dicarboxaldehyde (NDA) in the presence of cyanide ion (CN). The products of such reactions are cyano substituted benzisiondoles (CBI) which, in the case of AP and APM, exhibit high fluorescence quantum efficiency.

The objective of this study was to take a procedure and attempt to determine if the NDA-CN precolumn derivatization method could assay the Asp, Phe, AP, and APM levels in beverages.

Tables 4 and 5 (6,737) list the results obtained from the analysis of three different diet drinks using the aforementioned methods.

Table 4

fraction	Elution condition	% recovery AP	 APM
1	1.0mL of sample + 3.0 mL of 5% MeOH in 5 mM acetate (PH5)	97.0	0
2	3.0 mL of 10% MeOH in Acetate buffer (pH5)	0	0
3	6.0 mL of 30% MeOH	0	98.6
	Total recovery	97.0± 2.6	98.6±1.8

[a]n = 3

Table 5

Sample (n)[a]	Asp ± SD, μM	AP ± SD μM	Phe ± SD, μM	APM ± SD, mM
A (1)	22.9	58.8	25.2	1.68
B (2)	31.5 + 0.1	60.7 ± 1.0	42.3 ± 1.3	1.50 ± 0.06
C (3)	25.7 + 1.4	68.4 ± 1.3	30.9 ± 1.9	1.60 ± 0.0?
C (1)	27.0	70.5	29.2	1.64

[a] n = number of runs.

In summary, the study concluded that "NDA-CN derivatization methods were helpful for sensitive determination of Asp, Phe, and Ap by enhancing their sensitivity and, thereby, better detection of aspartame's degradation products." (2,1260)

This brief paper described some of the physical and chemical properties of aspartame and its chemical stability--discussing the factors affecting its stability such as pH, time, and temperature.

This paper then went on to describe several hydrolysis products. Finally, it reported several key studies outlining various HPLC separation methods in an attempt to quantify aspartame's decomposition products.

(Concluding paragraph summarizes the research paper. See pgs. 28-29, Fig. 15)

REFERENCES CITED

(Reference page format See pgs. 31-32, Fig. 18.)

1. Homler, Barry. "Aspartame Stability." Food Engineering. Vol. 5:127-128, May 1984.

2. Hayakawa, Kazuichi; Schilpp, Tanya; Wong, Osborne. "Determination of Aspartic Acid, Phenylalanine, and Aspartylpheny-lalanine in Aspartame." Jour. of Agricultural Food Chemistry. Vol. 38:1256-1260, April 1990.

3. Homler, Barry E. "Properties and Stability of Aspartame." Food Technology. Vol. 38:50-55, January 1988.

4. Tsoubeli, Menexia; LaBuza, Theodore. "Accelerated Kinetic Study of Aspartame Degradation in the Neutral pH Range." Jour. of Food Science. Vol. 56(6): 1671-1675, June 1991.

5. Graves, Donald; Luo, Siquan. "Decomposition of Aspartame Caused by Heat in Acidified and Dried State." Jour. of Agricultural Food Chemistry. Vol. 35:439-442, February 1987.

6. Tsang, Wing Sum; Clarke, Margaret; Parrish, frederick. "HPLC Methods for Determination of Aspartame's Decomposition Products." Jour. of Agricultural Food Science. Vol. 33(4):734-738, April 1995.

7. Stamps, Jeffery; LaBuza, Theodore. "An Ion Pair HPLC Method for the Determination of Aspartame and Its Decomposition Products." Jour. of Food Science. Vol. 54(4):1043-1046, April 1989. ***(Sources listed numerically as they appear in the text of the paper. See pgs. 31-32, fig. 18)***

Further Reading

(Indepth information or research referred to but not actually used is included in this separate bibliography page. See pg. 33)

Chess, C.A. and Gerson, D.J. 1986. *Spectroscopy* **1 (6):46-48.**

Daniels, D.H., Frank, K.L., and Warner, C.R. 1984. *Assoc. Official Anal. Chem.* **67:513.**

Prudel, M., Davidcora, E., and Davidek, J. 1986. *Jour. Of Food Sci.* **51(6):1393.**

Schertz, J., Monti, J.C., and Jost, R. 1983. *Lebensm Untersforsch und Technol.* **177:124.**

Sherman, J., Chapin, S., and Follweiler, J.M., 1985. *Amer. Lab.* **17:131.**

Stamp, J.A., and LaBuza, T.P. 1989a. *Jour. of Food Additives and Contaminants.* **6(4):397.**

The Awesome Science of Biology Series

The following page lists titles in this series which can serve as good examples of illustrated annotated reviews of current research. Peer-reviewed journals are explored by scientifically qualified authors who translate the technical jargon into terms understandable by beginning students. All sources are properly cited in the text and a reference list is provided. You can find details about these current and forthcoming titles on the website of Biotech Publishing, *http://www.biotechpub.com.*

Tant, Carl. *Awesome Green - The Explosive New Plant Sciences.* **ISBN 1-880319-05-5.** Softcover $17.95.

Tant, Carl. *Awesome Neurochemicals - The Essence of Sex.* **ISBN 1-880319-13-6.** Softcover $15.95.

Spickler, Anna Rovid. *Cancer Therapies - Awesome New Advances.* **ISBN 1-880319-22-5.** Softcover $19.95.

Spickler, Anna Rovid. *When Organs Fail - The Awesome Science of Transplants.* **ISBN 1-880319-23-3.** Softcover $19.95.

Trademarks

Claris Impact is a trademark of Claris Corporation.

Macintosh is a registrered trademark of Apple Computer, Inc.

UHUf Stick is a trademark of Faver-Castell Corporation, distributor for UHUf GmbH.

Other Books By Biotech

Science Fair Spelled W-I-N 2nd Edition - This book is for those who want to win! It is not a cookbook-students will have to think, organize, and plan. It is an honest and sometimes blunt assessment of both students and judges. It is about being confident and winning.

Paperback $19.95 ISBN 1-880319-12-8

Science Fair For Non-Scientists - At last here's help for that vast majority of often neglected students who are required to do science projects although their primary interests are not science. Those with too much pride for cookbook projects can learn how to apply scientific methods to almost any subject.

How-to and project ideas for artists, poets, dancers, writers, farmers, and all other non-science types can be extended to related scientific disciplines by those who wish. The author of the best selling Science Fair Spelled W-I-N guides scientifically uninclined students to success in their fields of talent and interest. They become potential winners because this is not cookbook projects — thinking is required.

Projects include everything from mud throwing to cow patties, food, dress, money, traffic lights, and politicians. The fact that specialized equipment is not required makes the projects ideal for homeschoolers and students in small schools!

ISBN 1-880319-16-0 Softcover $16.95

Radioastronomy On A Budget - Dr. Jay P. McDonald explains how to build and operate a KU Band (12 Ghz) radiotelescope from inexpensive off-the-shelf hardware. Complete instructions for use are provided. All this and more in a CD ROM format with hot key hypertext links.

ISBN 1-880319-21-7 CD $37.95

—and the latest title from the author of this book.

David Williams thinks science should not be all work, so he has provided Too Fun To Be Chemistry, a collection of games, puzzles, and demonstrations he uses with his students. The book itself is a complete guide for teachers. An added bonus is over 50 copy masters for quick provision of parts and templates needed. Even learning the periodic table and stoichiometry become fun experiences.

ISBN 1-88319-20-9 $24.95 includes copy masters

Glossary

Abstract - a summary

Article - a nonfictional, written work that exists as an independent part of a publication

Bibliography - a listing of sources used in a piece of writing, each including author, date, title, edition, and publisher

Cite - to give credit, within your writing, to the author of a particular study or quote. Different formats exist for this, such as "scientific," and "author-date" or "APA"

Documentation - the providing of documents or supporting references

Index - alphabetic listing of topics and their pages in a book; also, volumes listing appearance of a topic in different professional publications

Journal - professional publications reviewing current research in various fields

Literature Review - a description of scientific publications about a specific topic

Periodicals - a publication issued at certain intervals

Publication - published material

Reference - a bibliographic entry placed at the end of text; often misused as a synonym for "citation"

Index